MARGINALIZED!

How the Bible has been sidelined in our search for spirituality.

By Woodrow Michael Kroll

Marginalized!
How the Bible has been sidelined in our search for spirituality.
by Woodrow Michael Kroll

Printed in the United States of America

ISBN 9781628399370

www.xulonpress.com

DEDICATED TO:

John L. Benson

Paul Griffis

Frank M. Kroll

William Lane

M. L. Lowe

Roger Nicole

Marvin Wilson

Humble men who taught me to hunger
after God through His Word and to
find in the Bible all that I
needed to find Him.

ACKNOWLEDGEMENTS

There are many people who deserve to be acknowledged with regard to their influence on my life and the passion that I brought to writing this book. *Marginalized!* is dedicated to seven men, mentors all, who profoundly shaped my thinking about the absolute necessity and centrality of God's Word.

Rev. Frank M. Kroll was my father. A simple, faithful pastor under whose influence I grew into adulthood—influence both from the pulpit and in the home. My first educational stop after high school was Bible college. There a most gentle instructor, M. L. Lowe, taught me to love the Word of God. John L. Benson taught me the craft of preaching, actually preaching from the Scripture text and not simply using it to support what I wanted to say. Paul Griffis was my Greek teacher who modeled in the way he read the Word the importance of knowing what the New Testament writers meant by what they wrote.

My next stop was a Christian liberal arts college where I came under the influence of Marvin Wilson, my Hebrew teacher. He opened my eyes to the fact that you cannot adequately understand the New Testament until you understand the Old Testament. Another stop on my educational journey was seminary where I encountered William Lane who not only got me turned on to Pauline studies but demonstrated that unique blend of scholarship and heart. And then there was Roger Nicole, the brilliant Swiss theologian whose love for God through the study of theology caused me to want to know God better myself. These men weren't alone, of course, but they were God's chief masons who laid the foundation for my deep respect for God and His Word, and my equally deep love for both.

In addition, I want to acknowledge the team at Xulon Press who assisted in the preparation and printing of the book, and of course my wife Linda who became nearly husbandless during the months and months of research and writing.

The message of this book is critically important, but you would never have been able to read it had it not been for the influence of these people on my life and the assistance of these friends and family in getting this book into your hands. I am grateful to them all.

INTRODUCTION

Let the Journey Begin

Spirituality seems to be on the minds of just about everyone these days. Many of your friends and neighbors are on their own personal quest for something spiritual in their life. Likely, you are too; but, spirituality means different things to different people. To some, it's the pursuit of a deeper relationship with their Creator. To others, it's a connection with Mother Earth, and to still others, it's a feeding of the soul in ways the physical realm cannot, a connection to something greater than oneself, such as channeling, Yoga, Transcendental Meditation, etc.

In the last decades, however, with the rise of interest in spirituality has come a commensurate rise in confusion about spirituality. What is it? Why do we all crave it? Do we really need it? If so, why do we need it?

More to the point of this book, I have watched pastors, worship leaders and small group leaders in evangelical churches over the past two decades shopping around for newer forms of spirituality; looking for something that works, something that makes the path to spiritual maturity more meaningful and less difficult. They want something more contemporary than what they grew up with. They want spirituality with a buzz. Many churches have adopted things like Yoga or meditation. Some call for mystical practices, like stripping away your outer self to get to your inner self; but are these really the paths to spiritual maturity, or is there a better way?

Every book needs to have a purpose, or an author has no business wasting the reader's time. I have written *Marginalized!* because there is clearly a superior path to spiritual maturity that people in general, and many Christians specifically, seem to be missing. I want you, my reader, to know that there is a sure path to deepening your spirituality and it's not new at all. It's just neglected. It has been sidelined in the rush to find spiritual fulfillment through the practices I label as "the new Christian spirituality." More about this new spirituality later, but the path this book is about is the real path; the genuine path, often an undiscovered or underutilized path.

We will begin together to understand why God gave us a Bible and why His Word has always been God's preferred and required communication tool. We'll also investigate how such an amazing and necessary tool has been shoved aside, marginalized, in many of the current trends, toward spiritual growth. Ultimately we want to discover how receiving, reflecting on and responding to God's Word is the undisputed divine path to a spirituality that genuinely leads to God.

So my goal, and my prayer for you, is that once you have read *Marginalized!*, you will understand God's sure path to spiritual maturity and will crave to deepen your relationship with Him. After all, God wants your relationship deepened even more than you do.

You can enjoy a fuller, richer, more meaningful spirituality. If you're a Christian, you can move down the road toward spiritual maturity in your Christian life; and you can do this without becoming a mystic or a monk. That's important. It won't always be easy; the road to spiritual maturity is often filled with speed bumps that slow you down or detours that get you off track, but if you are relying on God's GPS, you will not go wrong. Discover true spirituality and the sure path that leads to it in the pages that follow.

So, let the journey begin.

CHAPTER 1

The Bible is How God Speaks to Us

Rhonda sat quietly in a women's Bible study group at church—feeling completely alone. The busy mother of three teenage boys came to the meeting looking for answers, yet now she was more confused than ever.

Tonight's topic: "Knowing and *Doing* God's Will."

All evening other ladies stood up one after another, testifying about all the amazing ways Christ was leading their lives:

"The Lord told me to go back to college and finish my business degree," announced an empty-nester.

"God is calling us to the mission field this summer," said a young wife whose husband just graduated from seminary.

Another woman broke into tears, and then said, "Jesus wants me to give up some bad friendships. It's hard, but I know I have to do it."

Everyone applauded and cheered. Rhonda slumped back in her chair and squeezed shut her eyes. *Okay, Lord. I'm missing something here,* prayed the forty-seven-year-old. *Nearly every woman in this room seems so clued into what You want for their lives. Not me. I feel completely clueless! Why can't I hear You?*

The weary mom looked up just in time to see half the ladies in the room hugging each other and the group leader raising her hands in the air. "God is moving through this church in a mighty way," the Bible teacher yelled into a microphone. "Daughters, mothers, and grandmothers are stepping out in obedience to what their Lord is telling them. And they're finding real transformation!"

Rhonda lowered her head again and stared at the floor. *Lord, what must I do?* She prayed again. *I realize my life is way too busy. I barely have time to pray let alone come to a Bible study. But what am I missing? What is it that these women have that I seem to have lost?*

Good questions . . . and maybe you've been asking them, too.

Don't worry, I won't make you—and others like Rhonda—read deep into this book without knowing God's sure path to spirituality and to Himself. I'll tell you right up front. I spent nearly 20 years in the classroom as a university professor, and during that time I became accustomed to hearing students wistfully say things such as, "It sure would be a lot easier to know God if He would just talk with us."

Coming to this faulty conclusion is exactly what slows down our progress in discovering God's sure path to spirituality. God does speak! He has not been silent. And Christians often do not grasp the forthrightness of this interchange. God has spoken to us—and continues to speak—through His Word! I want to underscore that statement. The Bible is where God speaks to us. Reading your Bible and paying attention to what you read is how God speaks to you.

Now before you put this book aside and say, "I read the Bible a couple of times and didn't get it," stick with me. If you read the next few chapters, you'll read all the way to the end of this book.

If you haven't yet grasped that God is not silent, that He has already charted the sure path for you, you may go on searching for God in the soup pots of the modern spiritual salad bar. And it doesn't matter who you are. I'm not just talking about young people, high school and college age, treading in dangerous waters here. It's easy for longtime Christians, parents and even grandparents, to look in the wrong places, or to stop looking altogether, or to fall into a routine of only attending church, or to jump into the practice of engaging in some other spiritual discipline without ever coming to grips with how we truly get close to God.

A. W. Tozer observed,

> "The facts are that God is not silent, has never been silent. It is the nature of God to speak. The second Person of the Holy Trinity is called the Word. The Bible is the inevitable outcome of God's continuous speech. It is the infallible declaration of His mind for us put into our familiar human words."[1]

In this chapter, let's investigate three foundational truths about God's communication with us: 1) God speaks with us; 2) God wants us to know what's on His mind; and, 3) Engaging with God's Word is the key to getting to know God intimately.

First, explore with me what the Bible says about God's conversation habits.

God speaks with us

Throughout Scripture, the God of the Bible is shown to be a God who speaks. The reason I want to begin here is because I think many Christians pay only lip service to this truth. We might agree conceptually that God speaks, and speaks through the Bible, but at the very same time we often treat the Bible as if it were just a story book. It isn't; it is God speaking to mankind, to us. It is a record of the mind of God to the minds of men and women.

The Bible repeatedly shows how God chose to speak directly to people, even to talk with them as a friend talks with a friend. The phrase "And God said" occurs ten times in the first chapter of the Bible alone. It is found 41 times in the Old Testament. But the similar phrase "The LORD said" is found in 202 verses in the Old Testament, and quoted four times in the New Testament.[2] That doesn't sound like God is silent to me.

Equally remarkable is the significant variety of people throughout the Old Testament God chose to speak with directly. Consider the following chart. (Please note that this list is representative and not exhaustive.) The point is that it's amazing to see how readily God spoke to people.

People to whom "God said" something personally

PERSON	SCRIPTURE
Adam	Genesis 3:9
Eve	Genesis 3:13
Noah	Genesis 6:13
Abraham	Genesis 17:9
Jacob	Genesis 35:1
Moses	Exodus 3:14
Balaam	Numbers 22:12
David	1 Chronicles 14:14
Solomon	1 Kings 3:5, 11
Hosea	Hosea 1:6
Rich Fool	Luke 12:20

People to whom "the LORD said" something personally

PERSON	SCRIPTURE
Cain	Genesis 4:6
Noah	Genesis 7:1
Abram	Genesis 13:14
Jacob	Genesis 31:3
Moses	Exodus 4:2
Aaron	Exodus 4:27
Joshua	Joshua 3:7
Gideon	Judges 7:2
Manaoh	Judges 13:13
Phinehas	Judges 20:28
Samuel	1 Samuel 3:11
David	1 Samuel 23:2
Solomon	1 Kings 11:11
Ahijah	1 Kings 14:5
Elijah	1 Kings 19:9
Micaiah	1 Kings 22:20
Jehu	2 Kings 10:30
Rabshakeh	2 Kings 18:25
Job	Job 42:7
Isaiah	Isaiah 8:1
Jeremiah	Jeremiah 1:7
Ezekiel	Ezekiel 4:13
Hosea	Hosea 1:2
Amos	Amos 7:8
Zechariah	Zechariah 11:13

The topics of conversation between God and mankind are as varied themselves as the men and women God spoke to in Scripture. For instance, God asked Moses what he had in his hand (Exodus 4:2). He spoke to Joshua about his personal importance to God and the people of Israel (Joshua 3:7). He communicated honestly to King Josiah about the forthcoming destruction of Jerusalem, the city God loved (2 Kings 23:27). God even related to Jeremiah a geographical prophecy about where disaster would come upon Israel (Jeremiah 1:14). The issues God discussed personally with people were both diverse and direct.

> **"God has spoken to us—and continues to speak—through His Word!"**

Sometimes in Scripture, God chose the indirect form of communication. Throughout the Old Testament, God is seen speaking through His prophets. Consider the following phrases as examples of how God chose men to be His mouthpiece:

"The word of the LORD came to Ezekiel the priest" (Ezekiel 1:3)
"The word of the LORD that came to Hosea, the son of Beeri" (Hosea 1:1)
"The word of the LORD that came to Joel, the son of Pethuel" (Joel 1:1)
"The vision of Obadiah. Thus says the Lord God . . . ." (Obadiah 1:1)
"Now the word of the LORD came to Jonah the son of Amittai" (Jonah 1:1)
"The word of the LORD that came to Micah of Moresheth" (Micah 1:1) [3]

Jesus: the mouthpiece of God

The New Testament does not record the same formula as the Old Testament ("the word of the LORD came to . . .") but it clearly accepts the veracity of these Jewish prophets. "For no prophecy was ever produced by the will of man, but men spoke from God as they were carried along by the Holy Spirit" (2 Peter 1:21).

Equally so, there is an important difference between the prophets of the Old Testament being the mouthpieces for God, and the singular Mouthpiece God chose in the New Testament. In the New Testament, Jesus was the voice of God in the flesh. John 1:1-2, 14 records:

"In the beginning was the Word, and the Word was with God, and the Word was God. He was in the beginning with God. . . . And the Word became flesh and dwelt among us, and we have seen his glory, glory as of the only Son from the Father, full of grace and truth."

What the Jewish prophets of the Old Testament revealed about what was on God's mind was the preface to what Jesus would reveal as the divine spokesperson for God. Hebrews 1:1-2 indicate that "Long ago, at many times and in many ways, God spoke to our fathers by the prophets, but in these last days he has spoken to us by his Son . . . ."

The four Gospel writers—Matthew, Mark, Luke and John—all crafted separate records of the life, death, and resurrection of Jesus Christ. They recorded much of what Jesus said, revealing both the mind of God and the incarnation of Jesus as the Word of God.

Luke described it this way:

"Inasmuch as many have undertaken to compile a narrative of the things that have been accomplished among us, just as those who from the beginning were eyewitnesses and ministers of the word have delivered them to us, it seemed good to me also, having followed all things closely for some time past, to write an orderly account for you, most excellent Theophilus, that you may have certainty concerning the things you have been taught." Luke 1:1-4

The writing apostles of the New Testament also claimed to have written what God revealed to them. "Paul, an apostle—not from men nor through man, but through Jesus Christ and God the Father, who raised him from the dead" (Galatians 1:1) claimed that God called him by His grace and "was pleased to reveal his Son to me" (Galatians 1:16). A Jewish rabbi turned preacher of the gospel claimed to have been caught up into heaven to hear "things that cannot be told, which man may not utter" (2 Corinthians 12:2-4) which, when he penned the substance of these visions which God would permit, was understood by his readers as the actual revelation of the mind of God. "And we also thank God constantly for this, that when you received the word of God, which you heard from us, you accepted it not as the word of men but as what it really is, the word of God" (1 Thessalonians 2:13).

As you can see, the list is getting long. The God of the Bible is a God who chose to reveal Himself through human spokesmen that He selected, and most especially through His Son, the Living Word of God, the Word who became flesh and lived among us. The Bible presents God not only as communicative but as communicating personally to mankind.

How God speaks to us today

But, one might ask, the prophets are gone. Jesus sits at the right hand of the Father in heaven—so how do we hear from God today? What is God's chosen means of communicating what's on His mind to our mind today? Ah, that is the question, isn't it?

Let's start with this important truth. The psalmist said, "With my whole heart I seek you; let me not wander from your commandments! I have stored up your word in my heart, that I might not sin against you. Blessed are you, O LORD; teach me your statutes" (Psalm 119:10-12).

The psalmist also knew that God's wisdom was revealed through His Word. "Your servant will meditate on your statutes. Your testimonies are my delight; they are my counselors" (Psalm 119:23-24). "Oh how I love your law! It is my meditation all the day. Your commandment makes me wiser than my enemies, for it is ever with me. I have more understanding than all my teachers, for your testimonies are my meditation. I understand more than the aged, for I keep your precepts" (Psalm 119:97-100).

Let me answer the question clearly and forthrightly. If you want to get to know God, you need to get to know His Word. That's where God reveals Himself today. "Let us seek to know Him in the Word," wrote A. W. Tozer. "It is in the Word we will find the Holy Spirit . . . for the Holy Spirit wrote this Book. He inspired it, and He will be revealed in its pages. . . . Let's open our Bible, spread it out on the chair, and meditate on it. It will open itself to us, and the Spirit of God will come and brood over it."[4]

How has the eternal God chosen to communicate with you today? Through His eternal Word, the Bible. If you genuinely want to get in touch with God, you'll still find Him in the pages of His Word. So, don't give up on it. The Bible is the sure path to God. Maybe you just need a new appreciation or a new approach to getting to know God through His revealed Word.

God wants us to know what's on His mind

As I will present in the next chapter, there is scientific evidence that reading your Bible is the paramount way for you to connect with God. Engaging God in His Word stands head and shoulders above everything else when it comes to moving Christians from spiritual immaturity to spiritual maturity.

Why is the Bible—reading it, metabolizing it (making it a part of our being), living it—so important in the process of spiritual formation? Equally so, why does marginalizing the Bible in any discussion of spiritual growth lead spiritual seekers even further from God? The simple answer is that the Bible alone records the mind of God to the minds of men. God wants you to know what's on His mind and you find out what's on His mind when you read, reflect and respond to Scripture. Let's unpack that concept a bit.

With all the talk today about people finding a vortex, sitting cross-legged in a sacred spot, visiting the departed, getting a word from the Lord, and having private revelations, there is still only one demonstrable, provable, reliable source for information about God: the Bible.

What gives the Bible authority?

When scholars talk about the authority of Scripture, they usually speak in terms of self-proclamation, unity, indestructibility, archaeological proof, fulfilled prophecy and other "proofs" of the Scripture's reliability. Those are all important topics, yet in this book, I am far more interested in presenting the position of supremacy that the Bible must hold in the process of moving a spiritually immature Christ-follower down the road toward becoming a spiritually mature Christ-follower. For, if the crown of authority in spiritual formation is placed on any other head, the Bible is indeed irrelevant to the process, or at least reduced to a mere contributing factor, one among many spiritual disciplines. Nothing could be further from the truth.

The Bible doesn't claim authority because it is the all-time best seller. Many books that have topped the *New York Times* best-seller list have enriched their authors financially but impoverished their readers spiritually. Sales figures do not create authority.

The Bible doesn't claim authority because it has been around for a long time. Other books are older than the Bible. *The Book of Kaqemna. A Treatise on Good Manners* was composed during the Third Egyptian Dynasty, during the reigns of Huni and Seneferu, circa 3998-3969 B.C. Or the *Per-em-hru*, more popularly known as the Egyptian *Book of the Dead*, dating from Egypt's Old Kingdom to Middle Kingdom and *Maxims of the Scribe Ani*, also known as the *Papyrus of Bulak,* both predate the Bible, including the writing of the Old Testament. Age alone does not guarantee authority.

> **"The Bible holds a unique place among religious and non-religious texts because it comes directly from God."**

What gives the Bible its authority is the character of God who authored it and whose character is reflected in it. Note how we can use many of the same adjectives and qualities when we describe the Bible as we do when we describe God. The recognition of this fact is essential to understanding the authority of the Bible. Consider the following examples of God's perfect character being reflected in God's perfect Word:

- God is perfect, and the Word of God is perfect — "This God—his way is perfect; the word of the LORD proves true" (Psalm 18:30a).
- God is to be exalted, and the Word of God is exalted — "I bow down toward your holy temple and give thanks to your name for your steadfast love and your faithfulness, for you have exalted above all things your name and your word" (Psalm 138:2).
- God is powerful, and the Word of God is powerful — "For the word of God is living and active, sharper than any two-edged sword, piercing to the division of soul and of spirit, of joints and of marrow, and discerning the thoughts and intentions of the heart" (Hebrews 4:12).
- God is life-giving, and the Word of God is life-giving — "You search the Scriptures because you think that in them you have eternal life" (John 5:39).
- God is efficient, and the Word of God is efficient — "So shall my word be that goes out from my mouth; it shall not return to me empty, but it shall accomplish that which I purpose, and shall succeed in the thing for which I sent it" (Isaiah 55:11).
- God is to be obeyed, and the Word of God is to be obeyed — "But he [Jesus] said, "Blessed rather are those who hear the word of God and keep it" (Luke 11:28).
- God is eternal, and the Word of God is eternal — "Forever, O LORD, your word is firmly fixed in the heavens" (Psalm 119:89).

Despite the similarities in the above list, we must be careful never to equate God and His Word. They are not one and the same. God is not the Bible, and the Bible is not God, and therefore we must never worship the Bible, and we can never equate a love of God's Word with love for God. Rather, the Bible has its origin in God. The Bible is the expression of God's mind and will. The Bible holds a unique place among religious and non-religious texts because it comes directly from God. Since it originates in God, the Bible's authority is related to the sovereign God's authority.

In Mark 7:1-13, God's Son clearly saw this authoritative relationship between God and His Word. Jesus was questioned by the Pharisees and teachers of the law about observing the traditions of hand-washing. Jesus' answer unambiguously distinguished the commandments of God from the traditions of men.[5] The implication was that not all 'religious' experiences, words, or traditions are created equal. The difference is origin. Some so-called authorities are of human origin but the Bible is of divine origin.

We all live under various levels of authority. But the Bible does not share its supremacy with any other authority. All claims for authority by experience, tradition or Church are claims that come from outside of the Bible and must rely on arguments that marginalize the divine supremacy of the Bible. It is this marginalization of the only book God ever wrote that has generated much of the spiritual confusion we see today.

Arthur Johnson in his book *Faith Misguided: Exposing the Dangers of Mysticism*, identifies the bottom line of authority when he says, "Scripture alone is seen as the final authority, because it alone, of all written or spoken statements, is the revelation of God."[6]

When God's Word must share authority with a church, an interpreter, "another testament," or with any other holy book, it is no longer the unique Word of God. It is simply a religious text, one among many, either to be accepted or ignored. God will have none of that. He never intended that we should either.

CHAPTER 2

The Bible is God's Sure Path and I Can Prove It

Deep. Dark. Dusty.

It's the eerie, alien world of a West Virginia coal mine. Your heart pounds as you descend into the blackness—with nothing but a headlamp to light your steps. Breathing is a challenge, and a fine layer of coal dust sticks to every inch of your body.

You pause to catch your breath. The stuffy air and damp, musty smells are ominous reminders: You are literally *inside* the earth.

But the men who work the mines don't come here for the views (or lack of them). They do it out of loyalty—commitment to their families, communities, and friends. They do it to earn a paycheck and to carve out a life *above* the ground.

Floyd Cox was one of those brave men. In the tiny mountain town of Pineville, West Virginia, the abundant seams of coal ripple through the landscape. These ancient deposits are his treasure. Coal heats his house and puts food on the table for him, his wife, and his three daughters.

"Coal is valuable, but it's not the *real* treasure of life," he was fond of saying. He often said this to anyone he met—from burly miners to the busloads of kids he drove to church on Sunday mornings. "It's not even nearly the most valuable."

He held up his Bible. "This is the true treasure."

Floyd was a man who *lived* God's Word. He trusted it, revered it, and was never ashamed to talk about it. As it did for the Psalmist, the Scriptures illuminated his path—brighter than the headlamp on the hardhat that he wore.

Through the many long years, this West Virginian had learned a secret from the mines—based in Scripture: Only Jesus Christ can provide the "coal" for our souls and lead us from darkness into the light of eternal life.

The Lord called Floyd home a decade ago. But if you happen to drive through Pineville and mention his name, you'll bring smiles to a lot of people's faces. Those who knew Floyd saw more than a hard-working coal miner. They saw a follower of Jesus Christ. They saw a man who walked, talked, and *lived* God's Word.

"We have the prophetic word more fully confirmed, to which you will do well to pay attention as to a lamp shining in a dark place, until the day dawns and the morning star rises in your hearts, knowing this first of all, that no prophecy of Scripture comes from someone's own interpretation. For no prophecy was ever produced by the will of man, but men spoke from God as they were carried along by the Holy Spirit" (2 Peter 1:19-21).

Floyd believed this with every ounce of his being. He knew that God's Word was reliable, relevant and absolutely accurate in everything he knew his Creator felt was essential for him to know.

Indeed, Scripture is "God-breathed"—as we observed in Chapter One—and it offers trustworthy guidance for just about every situation we'll ever encounter. Through the Bible, God teaches, rebukes, corrects, and trains us in right living. These ancient words are in fact amazingly timeless.

Marginalizing what matters most

Wise men and women like Floyd know the Bible is a sure path to spiritual maturity, but, sadly, God's one true and proven path has been marginalized. The dictionary defines marginalization as "relegating to an unimportant position." Today, the Bible is all-too-frequently marginalized in the search for spirituality. It is given lip service, yes; it's agreed upon almost universally by Evangelical leaders as a good path, but often this solution is only thrown into the mix of a mish-mash of spiritual disciplines. The Bible path to spirituality is often presented unenthusiastically as an afterthought, an unspoken given, or one solution only in a long list of many others. This marginalization of the Bible, about which we will say more later, may occur because engaging the Bible is neither new nor trendy. It lacks the spiritual sex appeal of Yoga or walking a labyrinth. It's something your grandfather might have told you, or your Sunday school teacher mentioned when you were a child. But—and this is key—it is the real solution to spiritual maturity, the only solution, the God-ordained solution. *People need to read their Bibles more consistently and more meaningfully.*

I can see eyes roll. Engaging your Bible by reading it more is simply not the dynamic solution people want to hear today; it's not magical or mystical enough. It's the archaic sort of counsel Charles Spurgeon might have given his congregation a century ago. Men like Floyd who view the Scriptures as the authoritative Word of God are in the minority, and a pastor would be hard-pressed today to create any sort of vibrant movement around Bible reading—right? Don't believe me? A friend of mine recently had lunch with the pastor of the largest and most cutting-edge church in their town. The pastor talked about how the church is growing by leaps and bounds, but lamented that most of the growth has come without spiritual depth. The pastor was searching for answers. Specifically, he asked my friend if he knew of any experience-oriented programs his church could adopt to help believers transition from spiritual immaturity to maturity. I wonder what reaction my friend would have received if he had simply said, "Encourage your people to dig into the Word more."

Yes, the solution to spiritual maturity is as simple—and complex—as people consistently engaging with Scripture. Please bear in mind that when I speak of Bible engagement I am not talking about simply reading the Bible. Bible engagement is more than reading, checking off a reading guide and saying, "Whew! I'm glad that's over with." Bible engagement refers to the practice of consistently receiving God's Word (by reading, hearing, etc.), thoughtfully reflecting on what has been read or heard, and obediently responding to the Bible in a way that both pleases and glorifies God. For more on what Bible engagement is, see Chapter 8 of this book.

This is the solution we need to rediscover. I say rediscover because there was a time in the church when engaging the Bible daily was a common spiritual discipline. My premise is that if Christ-followers have made only limited progress on the road to spiritual maturity, it's because they aren't reading and applying the Bible the way God intended. Sadly, we find today that a strange brew of mysticism and semi-monasticism has become the more popular method of getting closer to God.

I'm a Bible teacher. You expect me to say things like "the Bible is the sure path" or "people need to read their Bibles more consistently and more meaningfully." But is it just my assumption that consistent Bible engagement is the sure path to spiritual formation or is there any empirical proof that this is true? Would you be surprised if I said we can actually, scientifically, statistically confirm a direct correlation between the time, content, and caliber of people's engagement in God's Word, and their spiritual growth? The fact is, we can and you need to know the evidence.

The Center for Bible Engagement

Burdened about the plague of Bible illiteracy in America, in November 2003 I asked my board at Back to the Bible if I could create a research and development corporation under the auspices of Back to the Bible. My request was approved and The Center for Bible Engagement (CBE) was born. See Appendix A. Since that time the CBE research team has done thousands upon thousands (nearly 100,000 as of this writing) of scientific surveys in the areas of why people read the Bible or why they say they don't read it. We've surveyed both the general population and the Christian population. The research has been scrutinized by peer review and has been certified as legitimate, accurate and scientific. The findings are powerful, provable and provocative. Here are some results that have astounded all of us.

Within the last few years the CBE surveyed 40,000 respondents to examine the relationship between people's frequency of contact with the Bible and their personal behavior. In other words, does engaging God's Word actually affect the way people live their lives? CBE researchers asked anonymous respondents a series of questions about how frequently they engaged in such behaviors as smoking, getting drunk, gambling, pornography, sex outside of marriage, and destructive thoughts. Then people were asked to pinpoint on a scale from 0 to 7 how frequently they engaged their Bibles: 0 indicating never, 1 indicating one day a week, 2 indicating 2 days a week, and so on. To get the most complete picture possible, the survey included a mix of both closed-ended and open-ended questions and covered topics such as religious preference and beliefs, beliefs about spiritual growth and maturity, religious service attendance, and more. Researchers wanted to determine if Bible engagement was simply one of many indicators of deepened spirituality, or if there was something special about Bible engagement. Indeed, the survey showed that adults who engaged in other spiritual disciplines such as attending church or praying daily had a moderate reduction in the self-destructive behaviors mentioned above. By far, Bible engagement had the *most* significant impact on reducing these behaviors.

Bible engagement and behavioral change

Don't miss this. Overall, the survey found that:

- If a person engaged the Bible zero times or just one time per week, there was no discernible decline in self-destructive behaviors like smoking, getting drunk, gambling, pornography, sex outside of marriage, destructive thoughts, etc.
- If a person engaged the Bible two to three times per week, there was a marginal decline in such behaviors. There was a decline but it was not significant.
- But if a person engaged the Bible four or more times per week, there was a *dramatic* decline in self-destructive behaviors. Engaging the Word four or more times a week was responsible for life change that could be attributed to nothing else. [7]

Specifically, the odds of a person who engages the Bible four or more times a week engaging pornography were 61 percent lower than a person who does not read the Bible. A person had 57 percent lower odds of getting drunk. Gambling saw 74 percent lower odds, and sex outside of marriage saw 68 percent lower odds. These are not assumptions; these are the facts.

Now, I realize that spiritual maturity is about more than *not* engaging in risky behavior. But don't let these numbers slip by you too easily. Go back and look at them again. Behavioral change is the evidence of attitudinal change. The more we value our soul, the less likely we will want to do it damage. The two are clearly linked, which is one of the core teachings of the book of James. Spiritual formation is about thinking, speaking and acting more like Christ because down deep inside we are becoming more like Christ. By logical analysis, we can deduce that there is a clear correlation between engaging God's Word and therein discovering God's plan for spiritual growth and living out that plan in positive behavior.

As astounding as this is, there's more. Take a deep breath.

The power of four

The survey also showed that a person who reads the Bible four or more times per week had 228 percent higher odds of sharing his faith with others, 231 percent higher odds of discipling others, and 407 percent higher odds of memorizing Scripture. Now, if these findings don't grab your attention, you should check your pulse. And in a later study (November 2009), the CBE research team determined that greater Bible engagement was associated with a greater desire to grow spiritually, and greater likelihood of having a clear understanding of spiritual maturity.[8] These are not the ravings of a snake-handling country preacher; these are the verifiable results of scientific research done by qualified professions and certified by outside, non-biased professionals. The results are conclusive and irrefutable.

> *"To experience significant spiritual life change you must read or otherwise engage God's Word four or more times each week."*

Think about it this way: to be of any value to the Kingdom of God, spiritual formation must go well beyond moments of silence, an emotional feeling about God, or the practice of select spiritual disciplines. Spiritual formation must impact every activity of life and change the way we think and behave. If the meaningful engagement of the Bible jump starts our growth toward spiritual maturity, it should also prove itself to make a difference in our behavior.

The bottom line? If you want to grow spiritually, become more intimate with God by reading or otherwise engaging your Bible four or more times a week. There's more to it than this, of course, as we'll see later in this book, but this is where you start, and where most people fail. The solution is not as simple as checking off a box on a daily to-do list. Spiritual change does not come by following a reading plan and slavishly putting your time in God's Word. Rather, the key factor in becoming more like Christ and less like the world is significant, consistent engagement with God's Word, understanding it and making positive choices to apply it correctly. That's where the real difference is found, and that's the spiritual growth plan that has worked for centuries. Read your Bible daily. Read it in the right way and for the right purpose. Make your Bible reading meaningful because meaningful, consistent engagement with God through His Word will change your life. The facts don't lie.

A bedrock faith

Surely this survey raises additional questions, and we dare not sidestep these concerns. One of the core reasons people began the decades-back search for spiritual formation was that they observed the Bible being preached, but it wasn't changing lives—at least, not the lives they were observing. Take, for example, someone raised in a family where the parents were strongly religious and inter-acted with the Bible a lot, but the parents weren't particularly kind. Or perhaps someone attended a strong Bible-preaching church where the congregation split over something as petty as the color of the carpet. Or maybe someone gradu-ated from a Christian university where reading the Bible was stressed, but the university's spiritual climate was characterized by rigidity and rules rather than grace-filled living. The conclusion often reached is that the Bible doesn't work; that it is too hard core, and that we need to lighten up and realize we're imperfect people in an imperfect world, and we can't live and interact with God in the ways He's offered.

I strenuously argue otherwise. In any of these illustrations, spiritual immaturity was not caused by engagement with Scripture. Rather, faulty interpretation, faulty application, faulty approach and faulty obedience are among the real culprits. We live in a fallen world where misinterpretations and misapplications of the Bible do happen. That's just part of who we are as humans. If someone didn't find the answers to spiritual maturity in the Bible (or didn't live out the findings), it doesn't mean the answers were not there. It simply means they didn't find them. If we as Christ-followers believe the Bible is what it claims to be—a revelation of the mind of God to the minds of men—then we must trust it as a book of truth. We are on very thin ice if we acknowledge biblical directives but ignore them because "they didn't seem to work for our parents." That's tantamount to saying the Bible is not true. Some have done that and have looked for alternative approaches to spirituality but they needed simply were alternative explanations if engagement with Scripture didn't produce the level of spiritual maturity they would have liked to see in our parents, church, or university. Let's not throw out the messenger; let's reexamine the message and our application of it.

The story of a champion

It helps to remember that becoming spiritually mature does not guarantee that life will be perfect but it does create a bedrock faith in the goodness and sovereignty of God. I recently corresponded with a former student of mine from Liberty University where students were told, "We are here to train you to be champions for Christ." Believing this promise, students would graduate and be excited to change the world for Christ. Some were hugely successful in ministry and seemed to live charmed lives. But for many of these kids life didn't pan out the way they expected. My former student wrote, "I was told I'd be a champion, but that isn't true," as he continued his story.

After graduation he entered the pastorate. He married and had a family, but his wife of thirteen years was unfaithful to him. "She had been involved in an affair and contracted an STD, became severely depressed, and eventually committed suicide. I found myself a widower at age 35, a single father of two children and a devastated pastor." For four years, this broken man lived trying to make his way in ministry. Fortunately he met a wonderful Christian widow, married again and he is still pastoring a church, but for years he questioned God's goodness in his life. He concluded his e-mail with these sorrowful words: "I'm not a champion."

My initial response was sympathy. I told him how genuinely sorry I was to hear his story, that life doesn't always hand us the best of circumstances, and he's certainly been through a lot. Yet I challenged him with this: "Would you define a champion for me?" I wrote. "What makes you not a champion? Anyone who can survive the sort of thing you have—continue on with life, press toward the mark, and still be involved in pastoral ministry is a champion in my book."

So, yes, absolutely the solution to growing spiritually is for people to engage with Scripture four or more times per week. That can be proven scientifically. Yet, just because a person does this, it doesn't mean that life will be problem free.

A personal story

I can certainly relate to this personally. When my youngest daughter and her husband, Tiffany and Barry Percival, were expecting their third child, things weren't progressing as we hoped. An ultrasound showed our grandson's stomach was not developing on pace and his jaw was severely recessed. Doctors wondered at first if he had Pierre Robbin Syndrome, a birth abnormality that can be corrected by surgery. We did Internet research on the condition and were ready for it, reassuring ourselves that basically, by age five, a child with this syndrome's disorders can be fully treated.

But what doctors discovered later was something different. Our grandson's stomach was not developing correctly because the amniotic fluid in which he was encased was not passing through his system properly due to the recessed jaw and his stomach, nose, throat, and airway were completely closed off because of a much more serious genetic deficiency called Treacher Collins Syndrome.

There is no treatment for this condition. And that diagnosis was something we were *not* prepared for.

> *"Today we live the faith we've talked about all these years. God has not changed. He is no better or worse today than He was yesterday."*

My wife and I were out of the country on the day our grandson, Thaddeus, was born. We called our daughter to find out how the family was doing. After Tiffany talked to her mother, I got on the phone with my daughter. "Tiffany," I said. "Describe Thaddeus for me."

She did, and then began to cry. "Daddy what do we do now?" she asked.

Years later I look back on my response and believe it came from the Lord. The words that came from my mouth clearly weren't planned. They certainly don't reflect any sort of remarkable piety on my part. But I believed them then and I believe them today.

"Tiffany," I said, "today we live the faith we've talked about all these years. God has not changed. He is no better or worse today than He was yesterday. Things like this happen to a lot of families. They just have not happened to ours before now. If we really believe that God is good, that He is good all the time, and that all things work together for good to those that love Him and are the called according to His purpose, we must believe He is good through this too."

Challenges harden faith

When we came home, I shared the news of Thaddeus' birth on my daily radio program, *Back to the Bible.* The majority of the responses were positive and encouraging, but a few people asked things like, "How could God allow this to happen to you?" The implication was that, since I had devoted my life to serving the Lord, surely God wasn't being fair to my family and me. My immediate response was, "Who is in a better position to deal with this than a person of faith?"

Yes, we believe God is good, even through the challenges we face eleven years after Thaddeus' birth. His list of adversities remains daunting. Thaddeus was born without ears and is deaf. He doesn't have all the bones in his face, so his eyes droop. He breathes through a tracheotomy tube. We feed him through another tube that goes into his stomach. Thaddeus is mentally astute and mainlined in the public school system, but he's developmentally behind and has limited communication abilities. He has also been diagnosed with Obsessive Compulsive Disorder, ADHD, and autism. It's a perfect storm of disabilities.

The logistics of caring for Thaddeus are significant. My wife and I spend a great deal of time and energy helping out our daughter and her husband and family. My daughter meets about once a week with a different medical specialist. We meet annually with the entire team of doctors who plan our grandson's treatment for the next year, including surgeries (he has had 39 to date). I don't know why God has given Thaddeus to us, but I can say without reservation that he is a blessing. Thaddeus is totally loved by everyone in our family. Sometimes we fear that we love him more than the other grandkids because we lavish so much attention on him. He just needs more.

And yes, I'm so proud of my daughter and son-in-law. I don't know if I could handle the day-to-day challenges of caring for a child with this many special needs as well as they are. They continue to be strong, and I believe it's the spiritual quality of their lives and their walk with God that keeps them steadfast. Success and hope for them comes from being deeply grounded in the Word of God.

Certainly, it would be easy for someone in my position on the radio to dispense simple-sounding advice such as "read the Bible" in difficult times. But, rest assured, I'm attempting to live out in our family's crucible of testing any advice I dispense. Much of faith is the experience of not having answers, but not needing answers either. Spiritual maturity comes from living a life of active dependence on the Lord. I take comfort in the story of Job. How many times this venerable saint questioned God, but God never answered any of his questions. Not a single one. What Job had at the end of the book was a stronger faith in God than he did at the beginning, even without any answers.

Herein lays the danger. When people seek to become spiritually mature through non-biblical practices, when they marginalize the Word of God in their quest for spiritual maturity, they're building houses with materials that are neither strong nor trustworthy, and one day those houses are going to come crashing down in one of life's tsunamis. When personal crises come, they're going to find out that walking a labyrinth a dozen times didn't get them any closer to God or that sitting for hours in silence produced no answer. My fear is that unless they find the sure path, God's prescribed path, the disappointment will devastate their spiritual lives.

Errors, warnings, and answers

My aim with this book is to offer real hope and a good amount of practical ideas on how to meaningfully engage God through the Bible. Ultimately, I want to help people rediscover the sure path to spiritual maturity. In the pages ahead we're going to discuss what the Bible says about spiritual formation and how to develop true intimacy with God.

I want this to be a book about answers, more than questions. The truth must be told. And yes, if error about how to achieve spiritual formation lies within the broad array of sub-groups within Christendom, it must be addressed. So I'm going to give some warnings and talk about specific concepts, but I only want what's best and God-honoring for you.

My promise with this book is that spiritual maturity can be attained if pursued the way God designed. If we substitute anything else for God's design, we get whatever that substitute produces. God's instruction is that a substitute won't be as good for us as the real thing that He offers. God's solution to our spiritual searching is unpacked only from His Word. But that solution has been hijacked. Satan hasn't hidden God's solution; he has just fooled us into thinking there is a variety pack of "spiritual" activities that will lead you to God's heart. They won't.

Our task is to discern what is simply spiritual and what is actually biblical. Truly, there is only one way to distinguish between that which *sounds* spiritual and that which *is* spiritual. We need an outside criterion. We need a yardstick, a mile marker, an authoritative source to separate truth from error. I make no apologies when I say that the only standard that can adequately separate truth from error is God's Word. The Bible aids in our discernment of spiritual practices and shows us how to become spiritual without becoming a mystic or a monk. Ultimately, engagement with God's Word is the sure path to true spiritual maturity. I invite you along with me on a personal journey toward truth. It is the quest for spiritual maturity.

CHAPTER 3

The Bible's Top 25 Passages on How to Grow Spiritually

Gina was determined to do it. So she swallowed her pride, mustered up the nerve and went for it. Went for what? She had always wanted to play chess but had no idea where to begin or how to get over the intimidation of learning this game from someone. To her, chess players always seemed like cold intellectual types—deep-thinking, espresso-sipping, I.Q.-boasting snobs. Later she found out that wasn't true.

Getting a knack of the game was tough at first. After all, there was just so much to learn and to memorize, even before she could begin her *first* match.

For weeks, Gina watched her co-workers stare silently at the chess board during their lunchtime matches. Her friends would spend several minutes of intense thought before they'd move one little piece a mere space or two.

Sometimes, in mid-game, one of the players would lean back and disappointedly say, "Ah, you got me. Same time tomorrow?" Just like that, the game would be over. They were obviously able to look ahead and see how the game would play out.

Gina, on the other hand, was completely lost. Still, she had agreed to stick with her commitment to be a "chess-enthusiast-in-training" for at least two months. She carried around her beginner's chess board and pieces, which conveniently rolled up into one piece, everywhere she went. She spent every break, every lunch, essentially every down time familiarizing herself with the various pieces. A pawn could do this, a rook could do that, the queen was the most flexible and the king was to be guarded at all cost.

As Gina met with her chess teacher once a week, he was impressed with her progress and enthusiasm. At the end of her two months of lessons, the instructor reminded her that chess was a game of strategy. "It's easy to get hung up on the rules of engagement," he said, "or even a temporary victory, but that's not what it is all about. With time, you'll begin to see the next move, and the one after that, and the one after that. At that point, you'll truly be playing the game of chess."

It wasn't long before Gina started to understand what he was talking about. The goal and the rules are set. Every move prompts another move. One simple move early in a match can easily determine the outcome in the end. In other words, Gina had to learn to play the game while thinking ahead. Once she figured that out, she began to understand why chess players sit and look at the board for so long before making one simple move. They are trying to play out all of the possible moves in their heads.

Years ago, I saw the benefits of applying this same type of strategy to my life. There are times when I feel so overwhelmed and intimidated by life that I lose my focus. During those moments, it's hard to thoroughly think through my future decisions when I'm just trying to figure out the present ones. In fact, I came to realize that while I had a pretty good handle on the rules, customs and expectations of my own spiritual growth, knowing these things is of little value until I apply them on the chess board.

Here's what I did. I began by identifying my life goal, which is a growing personal relationship with God. As with chess, every decision I make today takes me either a step closer for further away from my goal. It is impossible to know where each battle will take me—but I do know the outcome. And I know something else: I need a strategy.

Discovering the strategy that works

While a number of the popular practices offered today as the secret to spiritual formation are not found in the Bible, there are many other biblical concepts that seem to be neglected in our spiritual seeking. Don't you want to know what God inspired the writers of the Bible to teach you about growing toward spiritual maturity? I know I do, and I think you do too.

And wouldn't it be great if you had a list of the top 25 passages in the Bible that would help you know what spiritual growth is, what is expected of you, and how you can grow to full spiritual maturity? Well, that's what comes next. Due to limitations of space we can only give cursory mention to these passages, but this will help you identify them so you can think about them, dissect them later, and put them into practice on your own. All these Scriptures are vital to us in the process of growing in grace and in the knowledge of our Lord and Savior, Jesus Christ.

The passages are listed in order of their appearance in the Bible, not necessarily in their order of importance. While their topics are diverse, they all contribute to a biblical understanding of what it means to be moving down life's road toward spiritual maturity in Christ.

The Bible's Top 25 Passages on How to Grow Spiritually

1. **Genesis 17:1,** *"When Abram was ninety-nine years old the LORD appeared to Abram and said to him, 'I am God Almighty; walk before me, and be blameless.'"*

To be blameless is not to be sinless. God does not require that we be sinless during our life on earth, but rather that we enjoy the kind of relationship with Him that means we have no skeletons hidden in our closet. To be blameless means we would not be embarrassed if the police raided our house and scoured through everything looking for incriminating evidence against us. To be blameless means we could invite anyone at any time to check out what we've been viewing on the Internet. It means to be so mature in our relationship with God that God is not embarrassed at how we walk before him. God's command to Abram was not to be healthy, wealthy or wise, but to be blameless. That's true of all spiritually mature people as well.

2. **Leviticus 19:1-2,** *"And the LORD spoke to Moses, saying, 'Speak to all the congregation of the people of Israel and say to them, You shall be holy; for I the LORD your God am holy.'"*

Even though in the New Testament the people of God are described as positionally holy more than two-dozen times, most Christians seem to struggle with practical holiness, day-to-day holiness. In a recent Barna Group poll, when respondents were asked to describe what it means to be holy, one out of every five adults said "I don't know." Only slightly less than a third of those who claimed to be born again believed that they were holy. Less than a third! Little wonder we have difficulty achieving the holiness that God demands of us if we can't even define what it is. God's command to Israel was not to be mighty but to be holy. Spiritually mature people are holy, set apart for God's purposes, not for their own.

3. **Joshua 1:8,** *"This Book of the Law shall not depart from your mouth, but you shall meditate on it day and night, so that you may be careful*

to do according to all that is written in it. For then you will make your way prosperous, and then you will have good success."

This is the quintessential power verse when it comes to the key to spiritual success. It's the only verse in the King James Bible that uses the word "success." Consider the relationship between the power words and phrases in this verse: *meditate, careful to do, make your way prosperous, have good success.* In this one verse is the formula for being a success in the eyes of God, and it all has to do with our relationship with the Book of the Law—the Bible. Success in God's view is not linked to money, mysticism or monasticism; it is linked to metabolizing God's Word to deepen our relationship with Him. Spiritually mature people are always people of the Book.

4. **Psalm 1:1-3, *"Blessed is the man who walks not in the counsel of the wicked, nor stands in the way of sinners, nor sits in the seat of scoffers; but his delight is in the law of the LORD, and on his law he meditates day and night. He is like a tree planted by streams of water that yields its fruit in its season, and its leaf does not wither. In all that he does, he prospers."***

Similar in intent to Joshua 1:8, the first three verses of the Psalms show the relationship between delighting in the Law of the LORD and constant meditation, as well as yielding fruit and spiritual prosperity. This is no prosperity verse; this is a promise that spiritual prosperity follows serious delight in God's Word. Spiritual formation is inextricably linked to the Law of the LORD, not to solitude, simplicity or secrecy.

5. **Psalm 119:47-48, *"For I find my delight in your commandments, which I love. I will lift up my hands toward your commandments, which I love, and I will meditate on your statutes."***

It is evident that the psalmist's approach to the commandments of God's Word is not one of mechanical drudgery but rather one of eager delight. Twice in these two verses he admits that he loves God's commandments—he doesn't just tolerate them or keep them out of respect for them. To this psalmist, loving God and loving His Word are one and the same. You cannot claim to love God's Word and marginalize it in your pursuit of spiritual maturity. If you want God to know you love Him, read and obey the only book He ever wrote.

6. **Psalm 119:97-99,** *"Oh how I love your law! It is my meditation all the day. Your commandment makes me wiser than my enemies, for it is ever with me. I have more understanding than all my teachers, for your testimonies are my meditation."*

The theme of meditating upon that which he loves continues for the psalmist. Now he fleshes out one of the ways he has prospered by engaging God's Word. It has given him more understanding than either his enemies or his teachers who had neglected the Bible in their knowledge. We cannot marginalize God's Word and expect God's blessing. It just won't happen. Likewise, we cannot claim we love God's Word and only read it without meditating on it. There's more to Bible engagement than most people know today.

7. **Matthew 4:4,** *"Man shall not live by bread alone, but by every word that comes from the mouth of God."*

Jesus clearly demonstrated the value of meditating on, memorizing, and metabolizing God's Word. The Savior had a command of the promises and prescriptions of God when He needed them the most—when He was tempted by Satan the most. You and I should learn the lesson here. Temptation need not overwhelm us by catching us off guard. It is something we can prepare for. All we must do is become familiar with the devil's devices by uncovering them in God's Word and with the Heavenly Father's promises found in the same place. You can't live by every word that comes from the mouth of God and relegate the Bible to a lower rung on your spiritual formation ladder.

8. **John 8:31-32,** *"So Jesus said to the Jews who had believed in him, 'If you abide in my word, you are truly my disciples, and you will know the truth, and he truth will set you free.'"*

We abide in the word of Christ by making it the rule of our life. In other words, obedience is the same thing as abiding in the Word. This makes us true disciples of Jesus and leads to genuine knowledge of the truth (God's special revelation which has its heart and center in the work of Christ). "Such knowledge, born of revelation and experience, sets one free." [9] But such knowledge is found only one place—in the revelation of Holy Scripture. To neglect your Bible in your quest for spirituality is to doom yourself wandering aimlessly in a spiritual wasteland.

9. **Acts 17:10-11,** *"The brothers immediately sent Paul and Silas away by night to Berea, and when they arrived they went into the*

> *Jewish synagogue. Now these Jews were more noble than those in Thessalonica; they received the word with all eagerness, examining the Scriptures daily to see if these things were so."*

The Berean believers are forever known for three things: 1) the eagerness with which they received the Word of God; 2) the carefulness with which they examined the Scriptures to see if what they heard from the teachers of the day was actually what God said; and 3) the regularity (daily) with which they examined the Scriptures they were so eager to receive. That's what I call metabolizing the Word. I've used that word several times already and you may wonder what I mean by it. Webster defines metabolism as "the chemical changes in living cells by which energy is provided for vital processes and activities and new material is assimilated." Is there a better way to describe how the Holy Spirit produces the spiritual energy received from assimilating what we read in God's Word so we can engage in vital processes and activities with regard to our faith? Be a Berean. Eagerly receive God's Word. Carefully examine it. And then metabolize it, making it a part of you, an integral part of your very spiritual makeup.

10. **Romans 8:29,** *"For those whom he foreknew he also predestined to be conformed to the image of his Son, in order that he might be the firstborn among many brothers."*

To be conformed to the likeness of Jesus Christ isn't an option for the Christ-follower. It's not like ordering off the breakfast or lunch menu at a fast-food restaurant. Before time began, God predestined us to be conformed to the likeness of His Son. The Father will have it no other way. Growth toward spiritual maturity is not an option. The alternative to being conformed to Jesus' likeness isn't non-conformity; it's disobedience. God knows our salvation isn't the end of our spiritual journey. It's only the beginning. Spiritually mature people don't end their quest at the starting point.

11. **1 Corinthians 2:6-8,** *"Yet among the mature we do impart wisdom, although it is not a wisdom of this age or of the rulers of this age, who are doomed to pass away. But we impart a secret and hidden wisdom of God, which God decreed before the ages for our glory. None of the rulers of this age understood this, for if they had, they would not have crucified the Lord of glory."*

The "secret and hidden" wisdom of God is not the wisdom promised by the Gnostics or mystics. It is the wisdom which a natural (unsaved) person does not accept (v. 14), in fact, cannot accept. It is a wisdom that is revealed by the Holy Spirit of God through the Holy Word of God. Whereas the pagan mysteries of the Greeks were revealed only to a select few, God's plan in its entirety is available to every person who will believe and obey His instructions (see also 2 Corinthians 4:3). Unfortunately, many who have easy access to the Holy Word do not often avail themselves of that access, and that stymies their journey toward spiritual maturity. They don't walk in wisdom but they wander in disappointment.

12. **1 Corinthians 13:11,** *"When I was a child, I spoke like a child, I thought like a child, I reasoned like a child. When I became a man, I gave up childish ways."*

The whole of the "love chapter" is a contrast between those Christ-followers who live like mature adults spiritually and those who continue to act like children spiritually. The apostle's point is that it is okay to act like a kid when you are a kid. But how long should anyone tolerate spiritual children remaining spiritual children? Unfortunately, far too many sitting in the pew on Sunday morning would be more at home in the spiritual nursery. But that can change, because spiritual formation is the by-product of pursuing spiritual maturity with dedication and persistence.

13. **1 Corinthians 14:20, "Brothers, do not be children in your thinking. Be infants in evil, but in your thinking be mature."**

Contrary to much of what we read in Christian "how-to" books today, genuine Christianity has as much to do with our mind as with our heart. Perhaps we have made far too much of a "head knowledge" and "heart knowledge" dichotomy. We are to love the Lord with all our heart, soul *and* mind (Matthew 22:37). Paul described his spiritual struggles as a "law waging war against the law of my mind" (Romans 7:23). The apostle challenges you to be transformed "by the renewal of your mind" (Romans 12:2). And to "Be renewed in the spirit of your minds" (Ephesians 4:23). As well as offering you this encouragement: "Let this mind be in you which was also in Christ Jesus" (Philippians 2:5 NKJV). We do need more than head knowledge, but we also need more than heart knowledge. God is a constant encourager for us to mature our minds by marinating them in His Word.

14. **Galatians 5:16, 25,** *"But I say, walk by the Spirit, and you will not gratify the desires of the flesh. If we live by the Spirit, let us also walk by the Spirit."*

Spiritual maturity is a matter of living in the Spirit of God, and letting the Spirit of God live out in us. The more we reflect the mind of the Spirit, the more we will live as the Spirit wants us to live. So how do we learn to live in the Spirit? And how do we learn to walk in the Spirit? It's not easy, but it would be much harder if we didn't have a divine GPS, a manual to guide us in Spirit-filled living. If we neglect that manual, the Bible, not only will we fail to live and walk in the Spirit but we will also be much more susceptible to gratifying the desires of our flesh. Failure to engage God's Word consistently and in a meaningful way is a lose-lose situation for anyone who wants to grow spiritually.

15. **Ephesians 5:1-2,** *"Therefore be imitators of God, as beloved children. And walk in love, as Christ loved us and gave himself up for us, a fragrant offering and sacrifice to God."*

To imitate doesn't mean to be a cheap knock off of the real thing. It means to see God as the example you follow, to make Him the bull's eye on your life's target. As R. A. Torrey has instructed, "God does not demand of us the impossible, He does not demand of us that we imitate Christ in our own strength. He offers to us something infinitely better; He offers to form Christ in us by the power of His Holy Spirit. And when Christ is thus formed in us by the Holy Spirit's power, all we have to do is to let this indwelling Christ live out His own life in us, and then we shall be like Christ without struggle and effort of our own."[10]

16. **Philippians 1:9-11,** *"And it is my prayer that your love may abound more and more, with knowledge and all discernment, so that you may approve what is excellent, and so be pure and blameless for the day of Christ, filled with the fruit of righteousness that comes through Jesus Christ, to the glory and praise of God."*

Paul's prayer for the Philippian believers was filled with themes we have already seen in the Bible's record of our need for maturity: knowledge, discernment, blamelessness, fruit of righteousness and more. We cannot unhook maturity and blamelessness from knowledge and discernment. We find both complementing each other only in God's Word. The key to genuine knowledge is the Bible. The key to real discernment is the Bible. The key to discernible blamelessness is the Bible.

And the key to being filled with the fruit of righteousness is the Bible. So why would we ever marginalize the Bible in our pursuit of spiritual maturity? Truly discerning people never do!

17. **Philippians 3:10,** *"That I may know him and the power of his resurrection, and may share his sufferings, becoming like him in his death, that by any means possible I may attain the resurrection from the dead."*

This is Paul's personal mission statement. And yet, too often, we fail to take note that the bottom line of the apostle's mission statement is not the resurrection from the dead or his share in Christ's sufferings. The bottom line for the apostle is to know Christ. The Greek word Paul used to express his desire was *ginosko*. It means to learn to know, come to know, or get to know. There is no implied innate knowledge here; if Paul is to "know" Jesus it will take effort, it will take study, it will take work, not mindless silence of effortless hoping. It will take that for you, too, to get to know Jesus in His fullness.

18. **Colossians 3:16,** *"Let the word of Christ dwell in you richly, teaching and admonishing one another in all wisdom, singing psalms and hymns and spiritual songs with thankfulness in your hearts to God."*

Did you notice there are four separate thoughts in Paul's prayerful benediction here: 1) the Word of God is to dwell richly in us, i.e. take up rich residence in us (that's metabolization); 2) the Word of God is to teach us and admonish us in its wisdom (that's education); 3) our response to the Word of God richly living in us is to be expressed in singing psalms and hymns and spiritual songs (that's praise) and 4) we are to receive the indwelling Word with thankfulness in our hearts toward God (that's gratitude). This benediction is all about God's Word and the benefits and expressions of having His Word become a part of us, be metabolized in us. It's all about the Bible.

19. **2 Timothy 4:3-4,** *"For the time is coming when people will not endure sound teaching, but having itching ears they will accumulate for themselves teachers to suit their own passions, and will turn away from listening to the truth and wander off into myths."*

My fear is that the realities these two verses describe have already arrived in our time, right now. People follow those teachers who suit their own passions, teachers who serve up salad bar spirituality, often laced with spiritual E. coli. They are oblivious to the truth; they often don't even care about the truth because they have developed their own truth. If ever there was a day to raise our voices against Bible illiteracy, it is our day. It is my observation that a lack of Bible engagement—taking it in and living it out—is the most debilitating trend the Church has seen in the last one hundred years. Little wonder we wander.

20. **Hebrews 5:12-6:1** *"For though by this time you ought to be teachers, you need someone to teach you again the basic principles of the oracles of God. You need milk, not solid food, for everyone who lives on milk is unskilled in the word of righteousness, since he is a child. But solid food is for the mature, for those who have their powers of discernment trained by constant practice to distinguish good from evil. Therefore let us leave the elementary doctrine of Christ and go on to maturity."*

These verses offer a compelling challenge not to remain spiritual infants throughout our lives, but to constantly be progressing toward spiritual maturity. Spiritual formation that doesn't lead to maturity is just empty talk. The goal of every Christ-follower should be that we consistently be watching the mile markers go by as we progress down the road to spiritual maturity. Much of what passes for biblical truth and spiritual teaching today is nothing more than spiritual baby food. It's a tragedy, really, that so many long-time Christians, including some church leaders, are stuck in spiritual infancy. God has so much more for us. The road out of spiritual infancy that leads toward spiritual maturity always runs through the Bible.

21. **James 1:4,** *"And let steadfastness have its full effect, that you may be perfect and complete, lacking in nothing."*

The scriptural standard for perfection (maturation) and completeness is to be fully developed in every biblical attribute of Christian character, to be complete in every area of the Christian life, even as Paul prayed for his friends at Thessalonica—"Now may the God of peace himself sanctify you completely, and may your whole spirit and soul and body be kept blameless at the coming of our Lord Jesus Christ" (1 Thessalonians 5:23). The goal is to become a whole man or woman, blameless in lifestyle, complete in Christ and mature in understanding. These themes repeatedly surface when the Bible speaks of spiritual growth and should be taken seriously by any who struggle spiritually to be all that God saved them to be. However, they are conspicuous by their absence in most discussions of spiritual formation today. You can change that.

22. **1 Peter 2:2,** *"Like newborn infants, long for the pure spiritual milk, that by it you may grow up to salvation."*

Who doesn't like a little baby? Babies are cute, cuddly and totally dependent on others to feed them. But who wants a baby to stay a baby all his life? Not one mother I know. We like babies, we just don't like people acting like babies when they are of adult age. The point of spiritual milk is not to stay on a milk-only diet long, but to use it to "grow up into salvation." The judicial part of our salvation—our justification—is instantaneous and unrepeatable. But Christians experience ongoing salvation from the time of our new birth until Christ returns for us and our salvation is consummated. Until then, we are to be growing in our salvation and that always requires more than milk. That requires metabolizing the meat of God's Word.

23. **2 Peter 1:3-9** *"His divine power has granted to us all things that pertain to life and godliness" (v. 3).*

This passage reminds us that God is our source. In order to be godly, you must never seek experiences that are not from God. By definition these experiences will not bring godliness. Godliness does not come by feelings but by "the knowledge of him who called us" (v. 3). The more you know of God through His Word, the more prepared you are to live a life of godliness. Therefore, you should "make every effort to supplement your faith with virtue, and virtue with knowledge, and knowledge with self-control, and self-control with steadfastness, and steadfastness with godliness, and godliness with brotherly affection, and brotherly affection with love" (v. 5). These are the qualities the Bible says keep you "from being ineffective or unfruitful in the knowledge of our Lord Jesus Christ" (v. 8). Don't be fooled by mantras, prayer words, mysticism or monasticism. It is rich knowledge that is the platform for godliness, knowledge that is found only in God's Word.

> *"There is no spiritual formation without biblical knowledge."*

24. **2 Peter 3:18,** *"But grow in the grace and knowledge of our Lord and Savior Jesus Christ."*

To grow in grace means to grow in our spiritual lives by means of God's grace, thus turning Christian commands into Christian graces. We grow in grace when we graciously grow more like Christ. But grace is only half the formula. We can only grow in Christian graces as we grow in Christian knowledge, in the knowledge of our Lord and Savior Jesus Christ. This knowledge is both progressive and personal. It is a continuing knowledge, one we get day after day, and it is a personal knowledge, one we discover on our own through God's Book. There is no spiritual formation without biblical knowledge. Like it or not, the less knowledge we absorb and apply from God's Word, the less spiritual we will be. It's as simple as that.

25. **1 John 2:14,** *"I write to you, young men, because you are strong, and the word of God abides in you, and you have overcome the evil one."*

Moving on down the road toward spiritual maturity not only means becoming more intimate with God, it also means becoming more adept at defeating the devil. What makes these young men strong? Not hours in the fitness center but hours in God's Word. What is our best defense against the strategies of Satan? Making sure the Word of God abides in us, stays with us, and changes us. The picture of spiritual formation in the Bible is always related to God's Word and to our growth in knowledge of His Word and its application to our lives. We should ask ourselves how it is that the current emphasis on spiritual formation has so little to do with God's Word when genuine spiritual formation has so much to do with it.

Mile Markers on the Sure Path

When we examine these 25 verses carefully, we easily see themes developing in regards to spiritual growth. Call them mile markers, like those little posts along the interstate that tell you how your journey is progressing. There are words repeated often, power words that describe what it means to grow in our relationship with God. The more of these mile markers you pass in your life, the further you are progressing on your spiritual journey. Here are ten of those mile-marker words extracted from the verses above:

- **Blamelessness** – any Christian winning the battle with spiritual struggles will not be clinging to sin, retrieving it when alone but hiding it when around others. Blameless people have nothing to hide.
- **Holiness** – any Christian winning the battle with spiritual struggles will have a good grasp of what God has in mind when He insists that we be like He is, holy, set apart from sin and dedicated to His righteousness and right living.

- **Engagement** – any Christian winning the battle with spiritual struggles will be engaged in God's Word daily, not only reading or hearing it, but also meditating on what was heard, metabolizing it into our very being, and acting upon it in the way we live before a watching world.
- **Delight** – any Christian winning the battle with spiritual struggles will not engage the Bible out of duty or guilt, but in delight, in response to our love for God and His Word. Reading the Bible is not an assignment; it is a breath of fresh air in a world stagnant with sin.
- **Abiding** – any Christian winning the battle with spiritual struggles will approach the Bible with the right kind of look—not a casual look (looking for verses that fit our agenda) or a critical look (looking for alleged errors or contradictions) but with a continuing look (abiding in the Bible, the written Word just like one abides in Christ, the Living Word).
- **Maturity** – any Christian winning the battle with spiritual struggles is consistently becoming more mature in our faith. We have not "arrived" but we are pressing toward the goal and making measurable progress that is easily discernible to all.
- **Imitators** – any Christian winning the battle with spiritual struggles views Jesus Christ not only as Savior and Lord but as example, as mentor, as the measuring stick for how to live the Christian life and please the Father in heaven.
- **Knowledge** – any Christian winning the battle with spiritual struggles possesses more than experience or feelings. The mature Christian recognizes the inescapable role of filling the mind with the things of God from the Word of God if we are to win the day spiritually.
- **Growth** – any Christian winning the battle with spiritual struggles is growing daily in the grace and knowledge of our Lord and Savior Jesus Christ. This growth is consistent, it is measurable, and it is demonstrable. It is evidenced by our moving down the road toward spiritual maturity.
- **Warning** – any Christian winning the battle with spiritual struggles is warned by God's Word that others who profess to know Christ often will migrate to those who endorse their already-held convictions, teachers, and authors who do not make them feel uncomfortable in any way. This is not the way to grow spiritually.

I mentioned that if we examine these 25 passages carefully we easily see themes developing, themes about spiritual growth. What we don't see in our examination of these key scriptures is anything about centering prayer, labyrinths, monastic living, icons, incense or almost any of the issues that are today's focus on much of what I label as "the new Christian spirituality." Is it possible that by marginalizing the Bible in our pursuit of spiritual formation we have also marginalized spiritual truth itself?

The Bible has a great deal to say about the Christian values and graces that come as a result of knowing God through His Word. But it has precious little, and often nothing, to say about the man-made approaches to discovering the heart of God that make up this new Christian spirituality, a spirituality that is an amalgam of ideas, sacred texts and practices, a spirituality that does not come from the Bible but from the spiritual salad bar being offered to us today. Perhaps it's time we left the mystics and monks to their own pursuits and sincerely began to ask, "What does the Bible say?" The secrets to winning the battle with any of our spiritual struggles are found only where God recorded them – in His Word.

CHAPTER 4

Maturity: The Quintessential Goal of Your Spiritual Journey

Ahush fell over the synagogue as a fiery Jew stood before the crowd. Today's speaker: a powerful Pharisee named Saul—the persecutor.

It was no secret how Saul felt about Christianity. He detested it. And everyone knew why he had come to Damascus.

For some time, Saul had been heard breathing out murderous threats against the radical members of the Way—the name given to the new lifestyle of Christ's disciples. Saul was leading a campaign of repression against them and was determined to bring down his iron fist on what he considered to be their unorthodox, even blasphemous, teachings.

Saul's eyes scanned the synagogue, studying the faces of his fellow Jews and members of the Law. The words unfolded slowly from his lips. "This Man. . . . This man they call Jesus Christ. . . . He is . . ."

Yes, Saul, get on with it, another Pharisee told himself. *Tell the crowd that he's a liar and a fraud. Tell them His followers are a bunch of lunatics who should be behind bars.*

Saul spoke passionately. "He is truly the Son of God. This Jesus, the One I thought was dead, is alive. I've seen Him with my own eyes. Those Christians are right!"

Everyone gasped.

"Isn't he the man who raised havoc in Jerusalem?" a voice shouted from the crowd.

"And hasn't he come here to take them as prisoners back to Jerusalem to stand trial before the chief priests?" shouted another.

Saul emphasized the truth. "This Jesus I am proclaiming to you is the Christ," he said. "Repent of your sins. Believe in the Lord Jesus, and you will be saved."

It was a miracle on the road to Damascus that changed everything! The stern Pharisee once bent on blocking the Way . . . now blazed a trail leading to the Way, the Truth and the Life. The feared rabbi once blinded with hate . . . now saw with a heart of love. The persecutor became the preacher.

What we can learn from the Apostle Paul

Since talk of spiritual formation is so widespread these days, we would expect the Evangelical community to be expert on what the Bible has to say about it. Yet while dozens of books have now been written on the subject, many of them are mysteriously silent about what the Bible actually says. This begs the question of why the Bible passages mentioned in the last chapter aren't playing a larger role in today's discussion about spiritual formation.

My guess is that there is a legitimate reason for this misguidance. It's because the phrase "spiritual formation" doesn't actually occur in the Bible. This doesn't mean the concept isn't there, but it does mean that it requires diligent study and correctly applied principles of interpretation for authors and spiritual formation teachers to lay their fingers on the appropriate set of verses to expound an accurate doctrine of spiritual formation. Most of today's spiritual formation books point people to passages about the heart, being at rest, being still, and listening to the still, small voice of God. But these texts are frequently misused and often horribly taken out of context.

So, what passages of the Bible actually refer to true spiritual growth, spiritual formation, and movement toward spiritual maturity?

Let's take a look at several frequently overlooked passages together, starting with Paul's ministry mission statement as written to the troubled church at Colossae.

"Him we proclaim, warning everyone and teaching everyone with all wisdom, that we may present everyone mature in Christ. For this I toil, struggling with all his energy that he powerfully works within me." Colossians 1:28-29

For the apostle, the bottom line of ministry was to *"present everyone mature in Christ."* That's the quintessential goal of spiritual life. To that end, Paul struggled with every ounce of energy he had. So why was presenting everyone mature in Christ so important to the apostle? Three things are evident from the text: 1) the *process* of Paul's ministry; 2) the *purpose* of Paul's ministry; and 3) the *power* of Paul's ministry (sorry about the alliteration).

Let's take a closer look at this passage together.

The process of Paul's ministry

The apostle often referred to himself by different ministerial terms. In almost every letter he wrote, Paul claimed in the first verse to be an apostle by the will or command of God (see, for instance Romans 1:1; 1 Corinthians 1:1; 2 Corinthians 1:1; Galatians 1:1; Ephesians 1:1; Colossians 1:1; 1 Timothy 1:1; 2 Timothy 1:1; and Titus 1:1). The only exceptions were Philippians, both Thessalonian letters, and Philemon where he appears to have personal reasons for deleting the apostle reference.

Paul's most descriptive verse about his ministry role is 1 Timothy 2:7 where he says, "For this I was appointed a preacher and an apostle (I am telling the truth, I am not lying), a teacher of the Gentiles in faith and truth." This triple role was important to Paul and may have been listed in order of importance as he saw them: a preacher, an apostle, and a teacher. In Philemon, his most personal letter and written to one individual, he simply calls himself a "brother."

The process Paul used in carrying out his ministry is clear, not only from the way he refers to himself, but also from the verbs he chooses to describe the way he does ministry: he proclaims, warns, and teaches everyone (Colossians 1:28). Three different verbs; three different activities. Take a closer look.

When the apostle said he *proclaimed* the mystery of God, he used a verb with a fairly broad meaning. In Greek, this word *kataggellomen* suggests a solemn or public proclamation. But the word bears a wider sense than Paul's favorite word for "preach," which in Greek is *kerusso* (v. 23). *Kerusso* means "to herald" or "to stand up and shout" (cf. Matthew 10:7; Mark 1:4; 1 Corinthians 1:23; 2 Corinthians 4:5; 2 Timothy 4:2, etc.) It's clear that as a preacher, Paul wasn't into "sharing" as so many are today. He was a herald, not a storyteller. In Colossians 1:28 Paul says he announced the facts of the gospel and then drew the net that leads to repentance and salvation.

The second verb in Greek Paul chose to describe the process of his ministry was *nouthetountes*. This is the verbal form of the noun *nouthetēs* meaning "an admonisher" (see Acts 20:31; 1 Thessalonians 5:12, 14; 2 Thessalonians 3:15, etc.). It's the word we often associate with "nouthetic" (correctional or confrontational) counseling.[11] It indicates that Paul had to take the Colossian believers aside and counsel them, even warn them about the creeping influence of Gnosticism in their church. Gnosticism was the pre-Christian and early-Christian religious movement that taught salvation comes by learning esoteric spiritual truths that free humanity from the material world. Essentially, Gnostics believed in salvation by knowledge. This belief placed the salvation of the soul in the possession of a quasi-intuitive knowledge of the mysteries of the universe. Gnostics were "people who knew," and they saw themselves as belonging to a superior class of people. Much of the New Age movement and, unfortunately, some of the spiritual formation movement, smacks of a rebirth of Gnosticism today.

The third Greek verb that characterized Paul's ministry to the Colossians was *didaskontes*. It means "to teach or instruct." This word is closely linked to the previous one. Paul found it necessary both to warn about wrong practice and to teach right doctrine. Teaching was so critical to Paul's understanding of progressing toward spiritual maturity, and yet it appears to be of such little importance for today's programs of spiritual formation. The greatest deterrent to being duped by wrong teaching is to know right teaching. The more we know the facts and intent of the Scriptures, the less likely we are to get sucked into a cult, a suspect Bible study group, or a church that is estranged from the Word of God.

Thus, Paul says in Colossians 1:28 that the process he used in his ministry to the Colossians was:

- to "proclaim" the gospel to them in all of its fullness;
- to "warn" them about the heresies of Gnosticism and other false teaching; and
- to "instruct" them in the truth of God. Paul wanted to be able to say of the Colossians what he had earlier written of the Thessalonians: "And we also thank God constantly for this, that when you received the word of God, which you heard from us, you accepted it not as the word of men but as what it really is, the word of God, which is at work in you believers" (1 Thessalonians 2:13).

In order to accomplish his ministry, Paul would need to use "all wisdom." But he was not mixing Greek philosophy, Eastern mysticism and biblical truth. Remember, he was talking to believers who had been infected with Gnosticism. The apostle was saying that he would not use the secret, esoteric wisdom of the Gnostics, but rather the wisdom that was available to all through God and His Word. "Wisdom" here is not *subjective*, the personal understanding of an individual, but *objective,* the quality of the truth itself (cf. Colossians 2:2, 23; 3:16; Ephesians 1:18; 1 Corinthians 1:22–25; 2:6, 7).

The apostle knew that if he was to present each of the Colossians mature in Christ, it would not take monasticism, mysticism, or mystery; it would take proclaiming the truth, warning against untruth, and teaching the truth.

Truth and wisdom: these are the tools of presenting everyone mature in Christ. They should be the tools of every pastor and teacher today because they carry God's seal of approval.

The purpose of Paul's ministry

Notice Colossians 1:28 again. The purpose of Paul's proclaiming, warning, and teaching was to "present everyone perfect in Christ." It's as if Paul was entering the presence of his Lord and Savior, Jesus Christ, and he was bringing with him all his trophies of grace. The apostle was unveiling his life's work in the Colossians and waiting breathlessly for the Master's "Well done." The words for "present" in Greek are *hina parastēsōmen* and suggest the last act of a lifelong process of shaping, molding, teaching, cleansing, and preparing the Colossian believers to be submitted to Christ for their eternal reward, and for Paul's.

We've all experienced this feeling at one time or another. We conceive of a project. We research the requirements for completeness. We assemble the right materials. We work long and hard at constructing, shaping, and molding our project. And when we have done all we can do, we present it to the judge or awards committee and wait in white-knuckled patience for the verdict.

Paul's investment in the Colossians had been extreme, especially for a tiny town a hundred miles inland from Ephesus and almost off the map completely, but his purpose was no different than it was for the larger church of Ephesus. He wanted to present the Colossian believers as his offering to Christ, completely prepared, completely matured, completely grown up in their faith, and as much like Christ as they could be.

Thus his ministry mission statement—*that we may present everyone mature in Christ*—is a model for all who are serious about spiritual growth, both in ourselves and in others of our family and friends. But let's focus more acutely on Paul's concept of maturity.

Some translations give Paul's ministry mission statement as presenting everyone "perfect" in Christ (NLT, KJV, NKJV, Young's Literal Translation, Wycliffe New Testament). The NASB opts for the word "complete" while others prefer "mature" (ESV, HCSB, TNIV, RSV, New Century). The translation committee of the NIV switched from "perfect" in the 1984 NIV to "mature" in the 2011 NIV. All are acceptable as long as we remember that "perfect" does not mean without sin, but rather means full, complete, mature, and completely grown. It is the Greek word *teleios* and implies being brought to an end, needing nothing more for completeness, or wholeness. In common usage the word denoted "full-grown," or "grown men," as opposed to "children" (Philippians 3:12, 15; Hebrews 5:1–6:1). This meaning is expressed many places in the New Testament (John 17:23; Romans 12:2; 1 Corinthians 13:10; 2 Corinthians 12:9; Hebrews 7:19; James 1:25; 1 John 4:17-18), as well as the Old Testament (Genesis 17:1; 1 Kings 8:61; 15:3; Job 1:1; and Psalm 19:7).

Also, we can clearly see the apostle's understanding of maturity and completeness in Ephesians 4:11-13, "And he gave the apostles, the prophets, the evangelists, the shepherds and teachers, to equip (perfect) the saints for the work of ministry, for building up the body of Christ, until we all attain to the unity of the faith and of the knowledge of the Son of God, to mature manhood, to the measure of the stature of the fullness of Christ." Put those words on the sticky side of your mind—equip, building up, mature manhood, fullness of Christ. They are important in the quest for spiritual maturity.

Again, we see it in Colossians 4:12. "Epaphras, who is one of you, a servant of Christ Jesus, greets you, always struggling on your behalf in his prayers, that you may stand mature (perfect) and fully assured (complete) in all the will of God." Again, note the words—mature and assured.

It ain't over till it's over

The New Testament church understood so clearly what many in the 21st century church haven't grasped at all—that the work of the ministry isn't finished when we assemble a crowd, however huge that crowd may be. Rather, the work of the ministry is only complete when we have accomplished the third third of the Great Commission ("teaching them to observe all that I have commanded you") and are ready to present those in that crowd to Christ, complete, mature and fully equipped. In many congregations today, the task has only begun and progress toward completion of the task is minimal at best, absent at worst. As former New York Yankee catcher Yogi Berra used to say in fracturing the English language, "It ain't over till it's over." The task of the Great Commission isn't over until spiritual newborns become spiritual adults, taught, discerning and ready to equip others.

Spiritual formation is all about growth toward maturity, or at least it should be. Primarily, it's not about worship, the spiritual disciplines, solitude, or silence, as important as these things may be as contributing factors. It is primarily about growth, about movement, about making progress down the road to spiritual maturity. Without that growth, everything else becomes practice but not progress. It's high time we began to talk seriously about the evident lack of progress on the road to spiritual maturity that is characteristic of so many churches today, even Evangelical churches.

Spiritual adults in Christ should no longer be babes in Christ (Hebrews 5:12-14), but should instead be mature and ripened Christians whose hearts are not only right but whose minds have been informed and shaped by the Spirit of God through the Word of God (Ephesians 4:23). Spiritual adults in Christ are full-grown men and women who are both mature and ever-maturing through daily engagement with God's Word (Ephesians 4:13).

Consider what the Bible says about the process of building up the believer in order to present him or her complete in Christ. There is a noticeable lack of this process in much that passes for spiritual formation today. But there is an equally noticeable lack of emphasis on engaging God's Word in a meaningful, life-changing way. Is it possible there is a connection? You decide.

The power of Paul's ministry

To say that the Apostle Paul was passionate about bringing people closer to Christ is an understatement. He was so passionate, nothing would stop him. He spent time in several jails—Philippi (Acts 16:23), Jerusalem (Acts 22:24), Caesarea (Acts 23:33), Rome (Acts 28:16) and more. He stared down an angry mob at Ephesus (Acts 19:21-41). He marched straight to Jerusalem knowing people there were waiting to kill him (Acts 21:4, 12). On his way to Rome he was shipwrecked in the Mediterranean and made it to shore only by clinging to broken pieces from the sinking ship (Acts 27:43-44).

Here's the graphic description of all that Paul endured just to do the work of his ministry. Compared to others, Paul said he was in . . .

"greater labors, far more imprisonments, with countless beatings, and often near death. Five times I received at the hands of the Jews the forty lashes less one. Three times I was beaten with rods. Once I was stoned. Three times I was shipwrecked; a night and a day I was adrift at sea; on frequent journeys, in danger from rivers, danger from robbers, danger from my own people, danger from Gentiles, danger in the city, danger in the wilderness, danger at sea, danger from false brothers; in toil and hardship, through many a sleepless night, in hunger and thirst, often without food, in cold and exposure. And, apart from other things, there is the daily pressure on me of my anxiety for all the churches."
2 Corinthians 11:23-28

If you imagine you can identify all these misfortunes, think again. The details of most of these experiences are not recorded in Scripture. Five times Paul received 39 lashes? We don't know any of these times. He was beaten with rods; we only know of Philippi (Acts 16:22-23). Stoned? We know that one—at Lystra (Acts 14:19). Shipwrecked? Don't be too quick. This is Paul's second letter to the Corinthians written, perhaps, A.D. 57, long before he took his ill-fated journey to Rome. We just don't know the details of the three times he was shipwrecked mentioned in this passage. For as many of the trials and hardships the apostle went through to help mature the Christ-followers he met, many more are left unrecorded in the pages of Scripture.

What we do know is that the mission to "present everyone mature in Christ" motivated him, drove him, demanded of him everything, and eventually took his life. To accomplish this mission Paul expended all the human strength God had given him. The language Paul used to describe the weariness of his efforts is heart-wrenching. Developing newborn Christians and helping them to move from infancy toward maturity took great "toil" (Greek: *kopiō*), wearisome labor (cf. 1 Corinthians 15:10, 58; Galatians 4:11; 1 Thessalonians 1:3) and even struggling (Greek: *agōnizomenos*), a derivative of the common Greek verb *agōnizomai* from which we get our English word "agonize" (cf. Colossians 2:1; 4:12). Taken together, these words give us a picture of a man who was working harder to "present everyone mature in Christ" than most of us would today.

Holy Spirit empowered

So where did the apostle get this strength? What was the source of power for his ministry mission to bring to maturity all those Christ-followers he encountered? This spiritual struggle was carried on, not through Paul's own natural powers, but with a Power greater than his. Clearly Paul realized that he was not doing this in his own strength, but "with all his energy that He (the Holy Spirit) powerfully works within me" (v. 29). It was spiritual power, not physical power. God provides the energy for fruitful ministry, not through popular energy drinks or food supplements, but through the power of the Holy Spirit. God energizes us for tasks we simply do not have the strength and stamina to undertake on our own.

Paul wants all of his readers, including you and me, to understand that through faith in Christ, the power of His Word, and the energy of His Holy Spirit, we can tap the same source of strength to accomplish more in ministry than can reasonably be expected. This is Philippians 4:13 in action: "I can do all things through him who strengthens me."

Paul was an evangelist, a church planter, an apostle, a preacher, a teacher and more. But what got him up in the morning and kept him up late into the night? The very thought that God might use him to "present everyone mature in Christ." This is the genuine goal of spiritual formation—an individual and corporate progression toward intimacy with Christ that does not come through mystics or monks but through the knowledge of who we are in Christ Jesus as expressed in God's Word. Where is this driving motivation today?

What can we know?

What can we know about spiritual maturity from Colossians 1:28-29? We know that we need God's Word to be proclaimed in its fullest form. We know we need to warn others about false teaching. And we know we need to instruct others (and be instructed ourselves) in the truth of God.

From Colossians 1:28-29 we know that spiritual formation is all about growth toward maturity, or at least it should be. It's about movement, about making progress down the road toward spiritual maturity.

And we know that spiritual formation isn't easy.

If we truly want to be spiritually mature, let's skip the "As seen on TV" approaches. The solution begins with prayer and doing what the psalmist did when he wanted to become more intimate with God: simply read God's Word and then do what it says.

"Teach me, O LORD, the way of Your statutes, And I shall keep it to the end. Give me understanding, and I shall keep Your law; Indeed, I shall observe it with my whole hear." Psalm 119:33-34

CHAPTER 5

Measuring Your Spiritual Maturity by God's Criteria

"Here on the mountain I have spoken to you clearly: I will not often do so down in Narnia. Here on the mountain, the air is clear and your mind is clear; as you drop down into Narnia, the air will thicken. Take great care that it does not confuse your mind. And the signs which you have learned here will not look at all as you expect them to look, when you meet them there. That is why it is so important to know them by heart and pay no attention to appearances. Remember the signs and believe the signs. Nothing else matters."[12]

Aslan, the great talking lion in "The Chronicles of Narnia," speaks these powerful words to a young adventurer about to set off on a quest. The life-changing wisdom leaps from the pages to reveal relevant truth in our own world as well. This, of course, is precisely the intent of the books' author, C.S. Lewis.

Aslan's words, in a very real sense, are the essence of Lewis' soul. The story he was telling carried a deeper, eternal message—one we all long to hear; one we're actually all helping to create with our lives. The signs he described point to the ultimate truth: the gospel of Jesus Christ. Aslan is a symbol as well, and much more than just the king of Narnia—he is symbolic of the King of kings.

Supposing, Lewis asked himself, reflecting on the nature of God, the sufferings of Christ, and other fundamental Christian truths, *that by casting all these things into an imaginary world, stripping them of their stained-glass and Sunday school associations, one could make them for the first time appear in their real potency. . . .*[13]

And so Lewis set out to do just that in *The Chronicles of Narnia*. And many years in the future (October 1963), long after the Narnia stories had been published, he wrote to a young reader who caught the deeper meaning of Aslan's words.

"If you continue to love Jesus, nothing much can go wrong with you, and I hope you may always do so. I'm so thankful that you realized the 'hidden story' in the Narnian books. It is odd, children nearly always do, grownups hardly ever."[14]

In reality, it took Lewis quite a while to realize the "hidden story" before he created "The Chronicles of Narnia." At age 17, Jack—better known to the world as C.S. Lewis—explained bluntly to Arthur Greeves, a Christian friend he'd known since childhood, "I believe in no religion. There is absolutely no proof for any of them, and from a philosophical standpoint Christianity is not even the best."[15]

Then, in September, 1931, the truth began to sink in—that is, with the help of his best friend, author J.R.R. Tolkien. It started on the grounds of Magdalen College, Oxford, England. God's Holy Spirit used Tolkien's faith and long discussion with his friend to move Lewis to faith in Jesus Christ as Savior.

Fifteen years after his declaration to Arthur Greeves, and a week and a half after coming to faith in Christ, Lewis wrote to Arthur Greeves again, this time with a very different outlook: "I have just passed on from believing in God to definitely believing in Christ—in Christianity. My long night talk with Tolkien had a great deal to do with it."

A number of years later, as C.S. Lewis was studying the New Testament and pondering what it means to be spiritually mature, he observed this: Everything that needs to be done in our souls, can be done only by God. Ultimately it is not the things we do that produces spiritual maturity but the things He has done for us. Here's what Lewis wrote in *Mere Christianity*:

> "Put right out of your head the idea that these are only fancy ways of saying that Christians are to read what Christ said and try to carry it out—as a man may read what Plato to Marx said and try to carry it out. They mean something much more than that. They mean that a real Person, Christ, here and now, in that very room where you are saying your prayers, is doing things to you. It is not a question of a good man who died two-thousand years ago. It is a living Man, still as much a man as you, and still as much God as He was when He created the world, really coming and interfering with your very self, killing the old natural self in you and replacing it with the kind of self He has. At first, only for moments. Then for longer periods. Finally, if all goes well, turning you permanently into a different sort of thing."[16]

Power phrases for spiritual maturity

God gave us eyes so that we might see, ears so that we might hear, a will so that we might choose, and a heart so that we might live. "I have come that they may have life," Jesus said, "and have it to the full" (John 10:10). But if you are to become who you were born to be, if you truly desire spiritual maturity, you must find what the Creator has set in your heart—just as C.S. Lewis did.[17]

While some people judge their spiritual formation by centering themselves or by ecstatic experience, the Bible never does so. Spirituality is better measured by the Bible scale of responsibility, not rhapsody.

This brings us to a second frequently overlooked portion of Scripture in the discussion about spiritual formation. It's Ephesians 4:11-16. While only six verses long, this passage is one that any pastor would be hard pressed to preach through on only one Sunday. There's just too much there. Really, to adequately treat these six verses, a pastor would need at least three months of Sundays because there are no less than a dozen power phrases in the passage, all of which relate to the real challenge of growing toward spiritual maturity—building the Church. If you want to move down the road toward spiritual maturity, you should at least be familiar with these power phrases.

Neither time nor space will permit a complete exposition of these dozen phrases, but let's take a "fast-forward" approach to the passage, aiming to be as thorough as possible within the constraints of this chapter.

Ephesians 4:11-16

"And he gave the apostles, the prophets, the evangelists, the pastors and teachers, to equip the saints for the work of ministry, for building up the body of Christ, until we all attain to the unity of the faith and of the knowledge of the Son of God, to mature manhood, to the measure of the stature of the fullness of Christ, so that we may no longer be children, tossed to and fro by the waves and carried about by every wind of doctrine, by human cunning, by craftiness in deceitful schemes. Rather, speaking the truth in love, we are to grow up in every way into him who is the head, into Christ, from whom the whole body, joined and held together by every joint with which it is equipped, when each part is working properly, makes the body grow so that it builds itself up in love."

Keep in mind that Paul's letter to the Ephesians is all about the Church—how the Church grows, what holds it together, and how members are to act. This epistle is the closest thing we have to an inspired "church manual." It was written in the context of the Lord Jesus giving gifts to His Church and establishing certain offices for the smooth functioning of His Church. It is not our purpose here to discuss those offices at length, but let's touch on them briefly before we consider the implications of the dozen phrases for building the Church.

What Jesus Christ gives to His Church

Before Jesus Christ ascended into heaven to take His place at the right hand of the Father, He promised His disciples, "I will ask the Father, and he will give you another Helper, to be with you forever, even the Spirit of truth" (John 14:16-17). The Holy Spirit was given to us to comfort us, help us, guide us and teach us, and the Holy Spirit's presence is the greatest gift Jesus could have left to us.

But He also gave other, lesser gifts, to the Church. They are apostles, prophets, evangelists, pastors and teachers.

- Apostles, in the strictest sense of the word, were the twelve men chosen by Christ who were eyewitnesses of His resurrection (Mark 3:14; Acts 1:22–24). They had power to perform miracles (2 Corinthians 12:12) as a means of confirming the message they preached (Hebrews 2:4). Their ministry was primarily to build a foundation upon which later centuries of the Church would be built (Ephesians 2:20). The apostles were not self-perpetuating. The word "apostle" is not used in the book of Acts after 16:4. As the need for apostles ended, so too did the office.
- Prophets, again in the strictest sense, were spokesmen or mouthpieces for God. At times they would foretell the future (Acts 11:28; 21:9, 11), but more often their job was to exhort, encourage, and strengthen God's people (Acts 15:32). God spoke through prophets—inspiring them with specific messages for particular times and places. Like the apostles, their mission was foundational to the Church.
- Evangelists were those who proclaimed the message as itinerant preachers, mostly going from place to place where there was no established work. They were much like the missionary of today. But it would be a mistake to think of them strictly as itinerant preachers. Paul's admonition to Timothy to 'do the work of an evangelist' is set within the context of a settled congregation, which presumably meant a ministry to believers and unbelievers alike.
- Pastors (shepherds) and teachers represent those who minister to a particular assembly of believers. Because the words "pastors" and "teachers" are linked by a single definite article in the Greek, it suggests a close association of functions between two kinds of ministers operating within the one congregation (cf. Ephesians 2:20). It may well identify the same person carrying out those two functions. If these are two separate gifts, they often work together in the same location, shepherding (counseling, guiding, pastoring) the flock, and teaching (instructing, mentoring, tutoring) people in a local church.

While apostles and prophets were used as foundational gifts for the early Church, evangelists, pastors and teachers serve the on-going Church to this day. In the first century, usually the evangelist founded the local church, the teacher built up the knowledge of the members, and the pastor provided the organization and guidance to the local congregation.

For our purposes, however, who these persons were is not as important as what they did. Why did Christ give these offices to His fledgling Church? What does Jesus want for His saints?

I remember when I was a little boy I used to make a birthday list every year. I knew I wouldn't get everything on the list I wanted, so I would pad the list to get the most I could. It usually didn't work.

But Jesus Christ has a list of the things He wants for us. It's a list of what He desires for our spiritual formation—and He expects to get everything. These are the power phrases we spoke about. In a nutshell—Christ wants us to be fully mature. What does that mean? Get ready to power up as we take a closer look at Ephesians 4:11-16.

What Jesus Christ wants for His Church

The Savior has already given the Church all we need to be spiritually successful. Anyone who feels spiritually inadequate hasn't yet grasped the fullness of Christ. Not that we are adequate in ourselves, but our adequacy is in Him. "In all these things we are more than conquerors through him who loved us" (Romans 8:37).

But the Savior also has expectations of us. There are things every parent wants for their children. As parents, we do all we can to see that they receive these things. But we also know that our children play a role in their own growth and success. Maturity takes personal effort, in addition to parental well-wishing. Likewise, Jesus wants certain things from His disciples. Ephesians 4:11-16 lists twelve of those things in power phrases.

#1. Jesus wants His followers to be spiritually equipped (v. 12).

The expression "to equip" or "perfect" the saints (Greek: *katartismos*) comes from a word meaning "to make fit or sound." It has the connotation of mending or repairing, or putting things right. In surgery, *katartismos* was applied to the setting of a broken bone. In the New Testament, the Greek verb *katartizō* was used for the mending of fishing nets (Matthew 4:21) and the restoration of someone who has lapsed spiritually (Galatians 6:1).

Jesus doesn't want His army looking like that iconic portrait by A. M. Willard of three rag-tag fife and drummers during the Revolutionary War (*Yankee Doodle, 'Spirit of 76'*). Jesus wants us mended, sown up, knit together and strong in the Word because the battle will be fierce and this is no place for untrained, ill-prepared spiritual sissies.

#2. Jesus wants His followers to do the work of the ministry (v. 12).

The ministry, here, is not a specialized occupation limited to people with professional training. The word simply means *service* and includes all forms of spiritual service for Christ. Gifted leaders are to equip the saints to do the work of ministry. They are not to do the work themselves but are to train, mentor, mold and shape Christ's followers for the work of ministering to each other in building up the body of Christ.

D. L. Moody said, "It is better to put ten men to work than to do the work of ten men." How true. The local church is not to be an arena for interested spectators, an aquarium for the fishers of men to admire, or a rest home for the spiritually tired. It is a training center for soldiers of the cross, an equipping center for those who understand they are saved to serve (Ephesians 2:8-10), and a strategic command center for preparing to invade Satan's strongholds.

#3. Jesus wants His followers to build up the body of the Church (v. 12).

Perhaps the most significant metaphor for the Church is the metaphor of the body. Corporately, all who are Christ-followers in this present age are "the body of Christ" (cf. Romans 7:4; 1 Corinthians 12:12-27; Ephesians 4:4,12,16; 5:30; Colossians 1:18; 2:19; 3:15).

Spiritual formation may begin in us privately and personally, but the ultimate goal of spiritual formation is to enable each follower of Christ to contribute to the growth, depth, strength, and life of the body, the Church.

The reason it is important for each of us to grow toward spiritual maturity is so we may assume our God-given role in building up the whole body of Christ and assisting others in growing toward spiritual maturity as well.

#4. Jesus wants His followers to live in the unity of faith (v. 13).

Ephesians 4:13 summarizes the reason gifted people are called to minister to all members of the local church in order to build up the body. It is articulated in the following four goals found in verse 13:

1) to enable the entire body to live in the unity of the faith (cf. Ephesians 4:3);
2) to enable the entire body to gain full knowledge of the Son of God;
3) to enable the entire body to achieve mature (spiritual) manhood; and
4) to enable the entire body to reach the measure of the stature of the fullness of Christ.

To be clear, the first goal is to achieve unity of the faith, not uniformity in faith. Often God's people understand things in God's Word differently, but that should never deter us from achieving a degree of unity in the faith. We are to be marked out as distinct from the world, not distinct from one another.

#5. Jesus wants His followers to absorb the knowledge of Himself (v. 13).

Christians are called to grow in faith to full knowledge of Jesus. "Full knowledge" (Greek: *epignōseōs;* cf. 1:17) implies that we start with little, but in moving down the road toward spiritual maturity we get to know Christ intimately by what we learn of Him.

The "Great Commission" of Matthew 28:19-20 is a three-pronged command:

1) make disciples;
2) incorporate them into the life of a local church (baptize them); and
3) teach them to observe all that Christ commanded.

Unfortunately, the third third of this command has become the stepchild of the 21st century church. The problem is that we get people to attend an event and we talk about the numbers. We get them to raise their hand and we talk about the numbers. We get them to sign a card and we talk about the numbers. We may even get them to come back to church, and again we talk about the numbers.

You want to talk numbers? How about the numbers of those who are fully discipled, and consistently and faithfully taught God's Word so they can be determined by Christ to be fully mature? Where are those numbers? Who's talking about them? We are strangely silent about them because, all too often, we don't have very impressive numbers to talk about here.

#6. Jesus wants His followers to achieve spiritual maturity (v. 13).

Spiritual formation is not complete until the goal of "mature manhood" (spiritual maturity) is achieved. In fact, "spiritual formation" may not be the best expression for what Paul is talking about here because it implies the process of forming as opposed to that which is formed. Jesus wants His followers to be complete, (Greek: *teleios*) in the sense of becoming adults as opposed to remaining infants (Greek: *nēpioi*). Paul is referring to organic completeness for the whole body, the Church, but while that complete maturity may be built one believer at a time, it is never fully achieved until every constituent part of Christ's body becomes spiritually mature. Jesus doesn't want His followers pursuing practices that lead to personal mysticism; He wants us to pursue those practices that contribute to the corporate maturity of the members of His Body—the Church.

#7. Jesus wants His followers to fully gain His stature (v. 13).

So how will you know if you have reached your goal of spiritual maturity? Only when you give evidence that you are completely mature as measured by the yardstick of Christ's full stature.

The Greek noun translated *stature* can mean "age" (as in John 9:21), and that may be the meaning here. We are pursuing spiritual maturity to reflect the "age" of the maturity of Christ.

How can we mortals possibly become as mature as Christ is? We can't, but we can allow His fullness to radiate out from our lives. When the temple leaders of Jerusalem interrogated Peter and John it was evident these disciples were uneducated, common men. But what astonished their interrogators was the recognizable and undeniable fact that "they had been with Jesus" (Acts 4:13).

When we are so filled with Christ and His Word that the world notices, we know we're achieving the manhood of Christ's stature.

#8. Jesus wants His followers to reach His fullness (v. 13).

The Savior's desire for us is that we be as complete as He is. Fullness (Greek: *plērōma*) has already been mentioned in Ephesians 1:23 in relation to the Church, but here it is the fullness of Christ Himself.

So what is Jesus' fullness? It is the sum of the qualities that make Christ who He is. These Christ-qualities are to be reflected both in our individual lives and in the corporate life of the Church, and the extent to which they are demonstrates the extent to which we have reached Christ's fullness.

While Christ's fullness embodies all that He wants to impart to us, it is painfully evident that we have only scratched the surface of what that is. But the Bible gives us some clues about how to reach Christ's fullness. "For those whom he foreknew he also predestined to be conformed to the image of his Son . . . and those whom he predestined he also called, and those whom he called he also justified, and those whom he justified he also glorified" (Romans 8:29-30).

There is an obvious continuum here with glorification being the point at which the full measure of Christ is reached. The question is where are you on that continuum? Are you making the progress you know you should be making? Have you moved closer to full maturity than you were the day after your salvation? If not, why not? And if you have made progress but not the progress you know you should have, why not? Is it possible that inadequate Bible engagement could be the answer?

#9. Jesus wants His followers no longer to be children (v. 14).

As I write this portion of this chapter I am sitting in the Atlanta airport waiting for a flight. Above me is an electronic notice board. A message just flashed on the screen about "infants in arms." Now, we all understand that when a newborn travels with his or her mother, the baby has to be held on the plane. They are "infants in arms."

But suppose when I entered the plane to take my assigned seat, instead of seeing the passengers neatly squeezed into their seats, all the passengers were holding another passenger in their arms. There they were: 130 pound women holding 200 pound men in their arms like little babies. How strange would that be? No stranger than what we observe in many churches today, even Evangelical churches. People who should be spiritually mature aren't. Even after many years in the faith, they are still "infants in arms." To bring a child into the world and not feed it so that it grows up healthy would be child abuse. To bring a child of Christ into the world (the new birth) and not feed it so that it grows up to full maturity is nothing less than spiritual child abuse. It's a crime the body of Christ should not tolerate but does.

Jesus wants His followers to grow up. He wants our childish fickleness to be replaced with spiritual perception and doctrinal stability. This is exactly what the apostle laments in 1 Corinthians 3. "But I, brothers, could not address you as spiritual people, but as people of the flesh, as infants in Christ. I fed you with milk, not solid food, for you were not ready for it. And even now you are not yet ready" (vv. 1-2).

Today's Evangelical church has more than its share of spiritual babies, Christians who are so Bible illiterate the pastor has to bottle- feed them instead of helping them feed themselves on the solid food of the Word. If you ask me, Bible illiteracy is not a problem in the church. Bible illiteracy is *the* problem in the church.

#10. Jesus wants His followers to stop being tossed to and fro (v. 14).

Employing the image of a ship riding out the waves during a bad storm, being tossed back and forth, not finding any stability or safety, Paul describes the spiritually immature in the same way.

Many in the church today run between this new teacher and that new experience looking for what is missing in their life. Their immaturity prevents them from understanding that what is missing is significant, daily engagement with God through His Word. Infantile believers, even if they have been Christ-followers for decades, are sucked in by the cunning craftiness of new doctrines energetically proposed by slick preachers or spell-binding authors.

The Greek word Paul chose for the craftiness with which such teachers advocate a new doctrine is *kubia*, from *kubos*, meaning "cube." It's a reference to throwing dice and is often synonymous with cheating. Believers who remain spiritual infants are not only cheating themselves of all the depth God's Word has to offer, they are also being cheated by the religious teachers and authors who contribute to their infantile paralysis. Perhaps worse, they are cheating Christ and His Church because they cannot assume the adult role in the Church Christ needs them to assume.

#11. Jesus wants His followers to speak the truth in love (v. 15).

Paul embarks on the great contrast between the spiritually ill-equipped—those who are still seeking the sensationalism of God in mysticism, and the mature believer—a person who has discovered the substance of God in His Word.

Jesus wants His followers not to sit idly by as their friends and family fall deeper into a sinkhole of spiritual ignorance. He wants us to speak up, to speak the truth concerning the causes for spiritual immaturity but to do so in love. Correcting an immature belief by alienating an immature believer doesn't build up the body. Crafty false teaching is generated by deception, but clearly biblical teaching must be generated out of love for the spiritually needy.

For the mature believer, our fundamental concern for the spiritual toddlers in our lives is not to treat them with disdain or disgust, but to treat them with the same demonstrated love God had for us when Christ died for us (Romans 5:6-8). We must always treat false doctrine as a cancer that has to be destroyed, but we must be equally careful not to destroy the weakened patient in destroying the cancer.

Apparently the need for spiritual growth lies heavy on the apostle's heart. Paul keeps returning to the need for Christ-followers to grow up. But he takes the thought even further here. When we speak the truth in love, it is so the spiritually-immature will abandon their childish beliefs and behaviors and "grow up in every way into him who is the head, into Christ" (Ephesians 4:15).

There is universality here. We are to grow "in every way"—in knowledge, purity, righteousness, holiness, grace, discipline and more. The Apostle Peter's final written command to his readers was, "But grow in the grace and knowledge of our Lord and Savior Jesus Christ" (2 Peter 3:18).

There is also directionality here. We are to grow into union with Christ and all who are in Christ. We are not to dig deeper into ourselves but we are to grow deeper into the reality of our union with Christ.

How do we know?

Now, I know I've spent a lot of your time on these power phrases—the things Jesus Christ wants for us. But they are important in answering this question: How does a person know if he or she is spiritually mature? The book of Ephesians demonstrates that spiritual maturity is more closely linked to responsibility than it is to rhapsody, to obedience than to observance. Spiritual formation is the product of time in the Word, not time in the whirlwind. It's not so much the exercise of the spiritual disciplines, (that's the evidence of spiritual formation) as it is the exercise of Scripture engagement.

Paul wanted us to know what he wanted the elders at Ephesus to know—that in Christ Jesus we already possess all we need to become intimate with God, all we must do grow up and begin seriously to pursue the knowledge of the holy. We don't get that knowledge from centering down, praying through or sitting in silence. We get that knowledge from serious time in God's Word, getting to know Him better and discovering all the "precious promises" He has for us—growth toward spiritual maturity being premier among them.

CHAPTER 6

Marks of Spiritual Immaturity and Maturity

If only we had a checklist of what to look for in spiritual maturity. If someone could just give us a list of dos and don'ts that we could use as telltale marks of maturity. Well, don't bother looking for one. It doesn't work that way. In fact, it would be legalistic to try and boil the process of being conformed to Christ to a list of dos and don'ts. Still, the Bible is not silent about what it means to be spiritual immature or spiritually mature. Do you know what it says?

A tiny acorn; no mighty oak

The deck on the back of my house faces west and receives heaping helpings of afternoon and evening sun. For years I've been bringing back nuts, seeds, pine cones, almost anything I could find from all over the world and I have attempted to get them to take root and grow in a big pot on that deck. Ninety percent of the time, nothing comes up (Yes, I know now some of these things will never become a tree). But some years ago I brought home some acorns from Reformers Park in Geneva, Switzerland, dutifully soaked them in a quick root solution, and put them in the pot. To my astonishment, a tiny oak sprouted from one of the acorns. I hoped someday to have a mighty oak from that sprout, sired from trees known to John Calvin: so I babied that infant tree all summer. When fall came, I took it indoors to weather the winter, and in the spring I put it back outside in the sun. At first it looked green and healthy, but as the months wore on, it turned brown and began to shrivel. It had plenty of water, but it was immature, and even though I gave it plenty of plant food, it was sickly because it would not absorb enough to grow into a mighty oak.

My little acorn sprout is like a lot of young Christians I know. They get a good start in their Christian life. They may even weather a few winters. But they fail to absorb adequate food to grow and thus they begin to brown and shrivel. In the end, they are horribly malnourished, and a mighty oak they will never become.

It is obvious that the writer of Hebrews was concerned about some of his Jewish Christian friends suffering the same fate. This passage in Hebrews 5, like so many others in the New Testament, is concerned with spiritual formation, actually with spiritual growth that leads to spiritual maturity. He was concerned that his friends were spiritually immature and were starving because their diet was that of newborns not of growing adults.

> *"About this we have much to say, and it is hard to explain, since you have become dull of hearing. For though by this time you ought to be teachers, you need someone to teach you again the basic principles of the oracles of God. You need milk, not solid food, for everyone who lives on milk is unskilled in the word of righteousness, since he is a child. But solid food is for the mature, for those who have their powers of discernment trained by constant practice to distinguish good from evil."* Hebrews 5:11-14

It is hard to believe that Hebrews 5 is almost completely absent in much of the discussion of spiritual formation, but it is. This powerful passage both identifies the causes of spiritual immaturity and the character of spiritual maturity. It is a portion of Scripture not to be missed in investigating spiritual formation.

Let's take a closer look together.

The marks of spiritual immaturity

Immaturity means something lacks growth or development. In a person, it means being childish, and lacking the wisdom or emotional development usually associated with adults. An immature person lacks wisdom, insight, discernment, coping skills, tact, and depth.

Unfortunately, *spiritually immature* is an apt description of much of Christianity in the 21st Century.

Like Ephesians 4:11-16 in the last chapter of this book, Hebrews 5 is an extended passage, and I will ask for more of your time to give it proper consideration. Why? Because it describes the recipients of this letter as people from whom better things would have been expected. Since they evidently had come to faith in Christ as Messiah and Savior some time before, they should have been mature in their faith, but weren't. The author was troubled by their childish immaturity and lack of progress on the road to spiritual adulthood. These Hebrew Christians were not much different from many Christians today.

In four short verses, the writer describes both the biblical marks of spiritual maturity and the marks of spiritual immaturity. According to Hebrews 5:11-13, there are six marks of spiritual immaturity, and then in the following verse, Hebrews 5:14, there are four marks of spiritual maturity.

Let's take a look at the marks of spiritual immaturity first.

1. Dull of hearing

Is this any way to talk to your friends? The Epistle to the Hebrews was written to encourage these Jewish converts toward a relationship with *Yeshua Hamaschia,* Jesus the Messiah. But the writer of this biblical book is also extremely candid with them in his assessment of their progress toward spiritual maturity.

Part of their problem, the writer says, is that they are a little thick-headed, dull of hearing. Written in Greek, the trade language of the day, the writer said the Hebrews have grown dull in their hearing (*nothroi gegonate tais akoais*).

There is a clear hint in the Greek verb *gegonate* ("You have become") that these Hebrew Christians had even regressed somewhat in their true spiritual perception. Especially through the teaching of St. Paul, the distinction between Christianity and Judaism became more and more eradicated. But the Hebrew Christians were inclined to cling fondly to their old rituals and religious practices for fear of losing them altogether. Perhaps they were clinging so tightly to their cultural identity as Jews they could not hold as tightly to their new identity as Christians. Like some Messianic congregations today, perhaps they had forgotten that in Christ "there is neither Jew nor Greek, there is neither slave nor free, there is neither male nor female, for you are all one in Christ Jesus" (Galatians 3:28).

For whatever reason, their ability to hear and understand had deteriorated through lack of use and so these believers became sluggish in their thinking. A universal side effect of neglecting God's Word is this same sluggish spiritual thinking.

2. Out of sync with God's clock

Failure to grow in their faith had also caused these Hebrews to be out of sync with God's clock. God is the ultimate time keeper. If you have ever visited the Royal Observatory in Greenwich, England, as I did several years ago, you know the value placed on correct time. It is here that Greenwich Mean Time (GMT) is established, and time zones around the world coordinate with it.

God, however, established a clock and calendar before time began that still governs the times in which we live. Genesis 8:22 reads: "While the earth remains, seedtime and harvest, cold and heat, summer and winter, day and night, shall not cease."

There is a natural rhythm to God's timepiece. In Ecclesiastes 3:1-8 we see fourteen opposites, each balancing the other to give parameters to time. "For everything there is a season, and a time for every matter under heaven. A time to be born, and a time to die; a time to plant, and a time to pluck up what is planted . . ." (vv. 1-2).

Did you know that God keeps spiritual time as well? There is a time, immediately after our salvation, for us to be novices, babes in Christ, immature and eager to grow. And there is a time in life, perhaps months or years down the road, for us *not* to be novices, babes in Christ, or immature.

The problem was that the Hebrews had failed to grow in the Word as God's clock moved forward. "For though by this time you ought to be teachers, you need someone to teach you again . . ." (v. 12). It was high time they had moved on to maturity, but they were stuck in spiritual infancy. They were out of sync with God's clock for spiritual growth.

Look around you. Many Christians today are equally out of sync with God's timing. They are spiritual babes long after their new birth, which is one of the marks of spiritual immaturity.

3. Need to be retaught basic principles

I remember my high school Latin teacher. She was a sweet lady but looked old enough to have learned Latin from Julius Caesar himself. She did her best to teach me *amo, amas, amat* (first, second and third person singular of the Latin infinitive meaning "to love") and I did my best to learn, but it was touch and go. It wasn't until a decade later that Latin began to make sense to me. As one of my seminary classes, I enrolled in a summer course at Harvard University entitled "Ecclesiastical and Patristic Latin." The title was enough to deter the fainthearted.

Our professor assigned only one textbook—Jerome's Latin Vulgate edition of the Bible. The first day he told each of us to open the Vulgate to Genesis 1 and begin to read. We looked at each other bewildered. He prompted us to give translating from Latin to English a try. As we came to a grammatical construction, he would stop and teach us inductively. Our professor claimed that every conceivable Latin grammatical construction occurred in the first eleven chapters of Genesis. Whether that is true or not, I don't know. What I do know is that even those of us who had Latin in high school needed to start from scratch with the basic principles of the language when we reached that class at Harvard.

That's the way these Hebrew Christians were. They had grown so little in their own faith that the writer of Hebrews knew he had to start from scratch with them. They were not naturally slow learners, but they had become lazy. They rarely read the Scriptures. They forgot the basic Bible doctrines they once knew and now they had become a biohazard of belief. The basic principles the writer talks about are from the Greek *stoicheion,* which refers to rudimentary ideas.

Did you know that most Sunday school curricula in North America run on a three-year cycle? That means that every three years, publishers of Sunday school lessons tend to repeat the same stories, principles, and lessons that were taught three years earlier. The age appropriateness of learning changes but the substance rarely does. Little wonder so many Christians today have never moved beyond the Bible basics and, in fact, need to be retaught those basics because they have forgotten them. That's indicative of spiritual immaturity.

4. Need milk not solid food

The idea that immature believers need milk because they cannot handle solid food is a frequent theme in Scripture. The Apostle Paul said of the Corinthian believers he could not address them as spiritual people but had to dumb down his message to them because "I fed you with milk, not solid food, for you were not ready for it" (1 Corinthians 3:2). Likewise, the Apostle Peter told his young converts "like newborn infants, long for the pure spiritual milk, that by it you may grow up to salvation" (1 Peter 2:2). Of course Peter did not want them on a long-term diet of milk; at some point they had to grow out of milk and begin to eat vegetables, fish, fruit, meat and more. Unfortunately, these Hebrews never grew that much and so years after their salvation they still needed milk and not solid food.

> *"The local church harbors Christians...who are stuck in spiritual infancy. They like it when the pastor's sermon is 'more taste and less filling,' but that's exactly the wrong diet for their spiritual needs."*

A purely liquid diet, such as a diet of milk, is inadequate for good growth in adults. It may keep you alive, but it will not make you muscular and strong. I know that all too well. I told you in the second chapter the story of my grandson, Thaddeus, who was born with a cranial facial genetic deficiency called Treacher Collins Syndrome. Because of his condition, even today as a young boy he needs to be fed a completely liquid diet through a "G-button" inserted in his stomach. Thaddeus is normal height for an eleven-year-old, but he weighs only a little more than 50 pounds. There is almost no muscle to his body. To me, Thaddeus is poignant living proof that a liquid diet, such as milk, is okay for an infant, but if you want to grow, you need more than that. You need solid food.

Unfortunately, the Evangelical church is filled with people who love liquid diets. The local church harbors Christians, like these in the Book of Hebrews, who are stuck in spiritual infancy. They like it when the pastor's sermon is "more taste and less filling," but that's exactly the wrong diet for their spiritual needs. They need more substance to their spiritual diet.

5. Unskillful in the Word of Righteousness

The spiritual anemia of these Hebrew Christians had a debilitating effect on their spiritual lives. The Bible often speaks of the need for every Christian to know God's Word, imbibe it, meditate on it, metabolize it, and make it a part of their lifestyle. For instance:

- Paul prays that God will give the Ephesians "wisdom and revelation in the knowledge of him . . . that you may know what is the hope to which he has called you . . ." (Ephesians 1:17-18).
- God commanded the prophet Ezekiel, "Eat this scroll, and go, speak to the house of Israel" (Ezekiel 3:1).
- The psalmist promised, "I will meditate on your precepts and fix my eyes on your ways. I will delight in your statutes; I will not forget your word" (Psalm 119:15-16).

We cannot interpret with absolute certainty the phrase "word of righteousness" in Hebrews 5:13 to mean the gospel or the Word of God. Given the context, however, that seems to be the most likely understanding. The gospel would be the word spoken by the Son (Hebrews 1:2) and the salvation declared at first by the Lord (Hebrews 2:3). Paul said he was not ashamed of the gospel for "in it the righteousness of God is revealed" (Romans 1:17).

As you grow in the Word, you learn to use it in daily life. As you find ways to apply the Word in every area of life, you begin to develop your "spiritual senses," that inner knowledge that comes from hiding God's Word in your heart. We often call this spiritual discernment. We all know that one of the characteristics of little children is that they lack such discernment. They make bad choices because they are inexperienced and untaught. Just as a baby will put anything into its mouth, an unskilled and immature Christian will listen to any preacher on television, buy any spiritual-sounding DVD, and attend any Christian conference or seminar, but will not be able to identify whether or not he or she is hearing truth or error.

Paul cautioned his young protégé Timothy about this very thing. "You will be a good servant of Christ Jesus, being trained in the words of the faith and of the good doctrine that you have followed. Have nothing to do with irreverent, silly myths. Rather train yourself for godliness" (1Timothy 4:6-7).

The antidote to falling for irreverent, silly myths is training ourselves in the words of good doctrine. The very thing that is missing in the lives of unskilled, infant Christians is also the very thing that will give them skill and help them to become mature, and that is the meaningful engagement of God's Word.

6. Possessing the characteristics of a child

My wife Linda and I were married in June of 1965. We have four married children, sixteen grandchildren, and one great-grandchild. Being "Papa" has been much more fun than being "Dad." But over these years I've had more than my share of opportunity to observe childlike behavior.

I use the adjective "childlike" because it is appropriate. It means resembling a child or marked by innocence and trust. When we observe the behavior of a five-year old we see the behavior of a person who has lived a sum total of 60 months in relative naïveté and innocence. They are childlike because they are still a child. And that is just fine.

But when you observe a twenty-five-year old, a person who has lived 300 months and they are still acting like a person who has only lived 60 months, we don't call their behavior "childlike"; we call it "childish." Childish means behavior that is befitting a child, marked by or suggestive of immaturity. Childlike is good; childish is not.

The longer we are in the faith, the less we should look and act like we just came to faith in Christ. These Hebrew Christians had been in the faith awhile and yet their behavior was childish. They acted like spiritual infants. They exhibited all the characteristics of newborns rather than seasoned saints. Spiritual maturity is marked by the distance we have come from our starting point as a newborn in Christ, not by the time we have invested in living the Christian life. As evangelist Vance Havner used to say, "How long you've been a Christian only tells how long you've been on the road, it doesn't tell how far you've come." Some Christ-followers have been on the road a long time, but they haven't come very far. That's indicative of spiritual immaturity.

No Christian has the right to remain a baby Christian. No Christian will grow in grace, moving on from infanthood to adulthood, who does not also grow in the knowledge of our Lord and Savior, Jesus Christ (2 Peter 3:18). No Christian can make any progress on the road toward spiritual maturity without meaningful engagement of God's Word on a consistent, daily basis. It's just that simple.

If you are exhibiting any of these childish characteristics in your spiritual behavior, don't be happy about it. This is not God's will for you. But don't be discouraged about it either because God has a plan to lead you out of your spiritual infantile paralysis into full spiritual maturity.

The marks of spiritual maturity

The bottom line with these Hebrew Christians was that they were still spiritual babies. They didn't have a hunger for stronger food from God's Word. At some point mature believers must stop frying fish for not-so-newbie believers and teach them how to catch fish and fry it for themselves.

Fortunately, the writer of Hebrews does more than simply identify the marks of spiritual immaturity. He also identifies the marks of spiritual maturity, establishing spiritual targets for his readers.

In some cases, but not all, the marks of spiritual maturity are just the opposite of the marks of spiritual immaturity. Spiritual maturity is comprised of:

1. The desire for solid food

While the spiritually immature person has no craving for anything but milk because it is easy to drink, tasty, and refreshing, the spiritually mature person understands that milk is insufficient for normal growth. It takes more. It takes solid food to build solid bodies.

In 1970 I was a student at the University of Strasbourg in France. My dormitory was two miles from the religion faculty building. The student eatery was just across the street from my classroom building. I had scraped enough money together to go to France to study (including attendant expenses), but I found that I also needed money while I was there. So, my first day in Strasbourg, I sold all my bus tickets and decided to walk the two miles to class every day as well as the two miles back to the dorm every evening. I also sold half my meal tickets. That meant I would load up on French bread and soup at Friday noon and not eat again until Monday morning. By Monday, I didn't want milk; I wanted solid food. I was hungry.

No mature Christian will be satisfied with milk after they have grown to the point their body needs solid food. It is only those who have not grown who find milk satisfying. One of the marks of maturity is the craving for more, for solid food, for deeper teaching, for more filling even if it means less taste. Hunger leads to maturity; satisfaction with less leads to less. In the church today, if we find ourselves satisfied with that hour and a quarter on Sunday morning, we can be certain we aren't hungering and thirsting after righteousness. In a week that has 168 hours, if a 40-minute message by your pastor will hold you over until next week, there is something seriously wrong. You are stricken with a lack of genuine spiritual appetite.

Today people often crave Gummi Bears because they are brightly-colored, squishy and tasty. But what they need is green beans because you cannot build a body strong in bones and muscles on Gummi Bears. What's true in the physical realm is equally true in the spiritual. People need green beans for growth, but immature Christians often settle for the theological and spiritual equivalent of Gummi Bears. Little wonder the 21st Century Church doesn't have a growth problem but is plagued with a depth problem.

2. Having the powers of discernment

What is the evidence that you are being fed an adequate spiritual diet—one that will help you grow in Christ and not just baby food that retards your growth? If solid food is for the mature, those full of age (Greek: *teleion de estin he setrea trophe*), what will be the evidence of that age? One certain evidence is the power of discernment, an ability that is blatantly lacking among milk-drinkers.

Here the writer skillfully makes a comparison of the physical with the spiritual. In a newborn, the digestive organs are barely developed and do not have the ability to assimilate more complex solid food like steak and asparagus. These digestive organs need to grow, be completely formed, slowly become used to processing more solid food, and eventually become weaned from just milk.

The same is true for our inner spiritual sense—our power of discernment. At first, a baby Christian tries to make sense of ideas even if they aren't godly. But the more of God's Word the young believer makes a part of his or her thinking, the more they ruminate over God's Word, the more they will be able to process ideas with spiritual discernment.

Those who do not feed on God's truth lack God's discernment. Often they must rely on what they glean from the Internet, the television, or their friends to determine right from wrong. This has led to the moral malaise we see ourselves in today.

3. Trained by constant practice

Building on this last thought, the writer of Hebrews explains that those who are spiritually mature, those who possess the powers of spiritual discernment, continue to grow "by constant practice" of these spiritual powers. Or, as my cardiologist would say, "You need the right combination of diet and exercise" to be healthy.

The proper diet for growth toward spiritual maturity is the solid food of the Word, not the simple ABCs that we learn from minimal contact with God's Word. And the proper exercise, once we have taken in and metabolized the solid food of the Word, is the implementation of that spiritual truth by thinking, speaking and acting in ways that please God and benefit those around us.

We don't take in the solid food of God's Word just to *fill* our hearts and minds; we take it in to *change* our hearts and minds. We digest God's Word to have the strength of manhood so we can live like men and women of God and not babies whining because we don't get what we want.

So, in the realm of the spiritual, our mental faculties—which at our new birth were exercised only on simple truths—should acquire by practice and proper feeding the power of seeing things as God sees them, distinguishing between right and wrong, discerning what are mature actions as opposed to immature ones.

The New Testament makes considerable use of athletic metaphors. Here the author speaks of our powers of spiritual discernment as being "trained by constant practice." In Greek it's an athletic term (*gumnazo*) meaning to exercise vigorously and without encumbrances. (It's the word from which we get our word gymnasium.) Just like running in the gym strengthens our quadriceps, hamstrings, hip flexors and more, exercising our powers of discernment strengthens our spiritual senses, moral moorings, ethical perspectives and more. But what if we run out of gas in our spiritual life? We do the same as we would if we run out of gas in the gym. We fuel up on more of the right kinds of foods—that which makes us fit, not fat. It's a simple formula: we eat, and we exercise. The more we exercise, the more fit we become. If this is true in the physical realm, doesn't it stand to reason that it is also true in the spiritual realm?

Proper diet and exercise translate to proper thinking and living. Our abilities to think like Jesus (have the mind of Christ) and to act like Jesus (live as Christ lived) are tied to our eating more solid food and constantly exercising our ability to discern according to God's truth.

4. Possessing the ability to distinguish good from evil

In our postmodern world nothing is ever considered black or white; everything is gray and you get to choose your own shade of gray. Nothing is good or bad;

it's whether it's good for you or bad for you. Nothing is right or wrong; it's whether it's right for you or wrong for you. But our postmodern world is a gullible world, to say the least. Some things are just plain good: food, shelter and a loving family are good; living hungry on the streets all alone is bad. Some things are just plain right: justice and righteousness are right; injustice and unrighteousness are wrong. Some things are black and some things are white. Coal is black; snow is white. It's not that coal is better or worse than snow. You can't heat your house in the winter with snow, just as you can't cover an ugly cornfield with coal and make it beautiful in winter. These things are just different and calling them gray won't make them so.

In the spiritual, ethical, and moral world, we need to be able to discern good from evil. There is an inner law of right and wrong we call our conscience, but it doesn't cover all the bases and it doesn't cover any of them adequately. We need more. Fortunately, we have more—we have the mind of God revealed in the Word of God. But the infantile believer doesn't possess the ability to distinguish good from evil, right from wrong. It was this inability to discriminate that sucked these Hebrew Christians into strange doctrine. The author warned them, "Do not be led away by diverse and strange teachings" (Hebrews 13:9).

That's a warning the Church of the 21st century would do well to heed. Until we become convinced of the importance of being fruitfully engaged in God's Word and stop looking for spirituality to come from the mystical East or the monastic desert, we will continue to be misled into thinking that simply practicing the spiritual disciplines is spiritual depth. The spiritual disciplines are important, but they are not the cause of spiritual growth; they are the evidence of it.[18]

Food for the mature

What does it mean to be truly spiritually mature? Nowhere in the Bible does it say that maturity springs from chanting the same word over and over again or peeling away the false self or walking a labyrinth.

Real spiritual depth comes from God's Word. The Bible is the key. Genuine spiritual progress from immaturity to maturity comes from good diet and plenty of exercise. Without the incalculable benefit of metabolizing into our being the mind of God through the Word of God and the exercise of God's Word in our daily walk, spiritual formation is just a bubble floating toward a waiting pin.

I find much encouragement in Psalm 119, the longest psalm in the Bible. Verses 9-16 are particularly helpful in this area. Take them in and live them out and you'll make some progress down the road toward spiritual maturity.

"How can a young man keep his way pure? By guarding it according to your word. With my whole heart I seek you, let me not wander from your commandments! I have stored up your word in my heart, that I might not sin against you. Blessed are you, O LORD, teach me your statutes! With my lips I declare all the rules of your mouth. In the way of your testimonies I delight as much as in all riches. I will meditate on your precepts and fix my eyes on your ways. I will delight in your statutes; I will not forget your word."

CHAPTER 7

The Spiritual Formation Game Changer

By now you've noticed how much Scripture I've used in the first six chapters of this book. There's a reason for that. If engaging the Bible is the key to spiritual growth, engaging the Bible is also the key to correct thinking about spiritual growth. I've used many references to Scripture because I believe in the Bible's unique authority over the Christian's life. Besides, the Bible has a great deal to say about growing toward spiritually maturity that I don't find in the plethora of books available on spirituality. If the Bible has the answer, why don't we apply it more frequently to our questions? Is it because we don't know as much about what's in the Bible as we should? And if we know it's in there, are we such infrequent visitors to the Holy Text that we can't find what we know is in there?

While we have plodded through several key passages in the New Testament that help us understand God's take on spiritual formation, we really need a game changer. A game changer is one incident, one play that changes the whole complexion of the game.

It was October, 2011. The Nebraska Cornhuskers were playing a very good Ohio State team at home in Lincoln, Nebraska. It was homecoming. It should have been a happy autumn football Saturday afternoon but the Huskers were lackluster at best and OSU was leading by a score of 27 to 6. We Husker fans just wanted it to be over. It was embarrassing. But then something almost miraculous happened. With the Ohio State quarterback carrying the ball, Nebraska linebacker Lavonte David stripped the ball from the quarterback's hands and it became Nebraska's ball late in the third quarter. With twenty-eight unanswered points later, Nebraska had scored the greatest come-from-behind win in school history. The offense looked energized, as did the defense. But it was that one play by the linebacker that changed the whole course of the game.

That's what's needed in our spiritual journey. We've investigated many Bible passages that describe the "what" and "how" of progressing toward spiritual maturity from God's point of view. What we need is a game changer, a passage that makes it unmistakably clear that engaging God in His Word leads to the lifestyle changes we saw proven by the scientific research of The Center for Bible Engagement in Chapter 2. It would be hard to pinpoint a single "most important" passage in the prolific writings of the Apostle Paul. We could argue for so many. But if there is a game changer and if I were pressed to choose one, it would be Romans 12:1-2.

"I appeal to you therefore, brothers, by the mercies of God, to present your bodies as a living sacrifice, holy and acceptable to God, which is your spiritual worship. Do not be conformed to this world, but be transformed by the renewal of your mind, that by testing you may discern what is the will of God, what is good and acceptable and perfect."

I call this passage a game changer because the key to genuine spiritual formation is transformation, and the key to transformation is a fundamental change both in who we are and what we do. Transformation is what eradicates spiritual immaturity and promotes spiritual maturity. Nowhere is this dual aspect of transformation better seen than in Paul's admonitions of Romans 12:1-2.

So, as we've done with Ephesians 4 and Hebrews 5, let's explore this classic passage more in depth, keeping an eye out for transformational insights. Consider with me how things must be done differently if we are to make progress on our journey toward spiritual maturity, because, really, the key to genuine spiritual formation is not emptying the mind, it's transforming the mind. When that happens, transformed behavior will follow.

The urgency of change

It is evident from the first word of these verses that Paul's thoughts are in transition. The first eleven chapters of Romans have been exposition. Now Paul turns to exhortation. "Therefore" establishes a connection with his entire foregoing presentation, but the connection is particularly close with Romans 6:13 and 19. The apostle begins now to "urge" his readers instead of simply instructing them. While instruction is important to transformation, change is the key. Based on what we know, we must change what we do.

In each of Paul's letters he follows the same writing style. First, he establishes truth that becomes doctrine. Then he urges his readers to make application of that truth. Doctrine becomes duty. Talk becomes walk. "What" becomes "how."

This we see in Romans 12:1-2. Consider with me that Romans 12:1 contains 5 essential elements.

1) a passionate appeal: *"I appeal to you therefore, brothers"*
2) persuasive reason: *"by the mercies of God"*
3) an extraordinary command: *"to present your bodies as a living sacrifice"*
4) a vivid description: *"holy and acceptable to God"*
5) a compelling rationale: *"which is your spiritual worship"*

Paul's appeal to the Romans is both heartfelt and genuine. The Greek word "appeal" is *parakaleo*. It's a construct word composed of two smaller words meaning "to call alongside." It means to urge, beseech, exhort or admonish. It's a tender word. As a preacher and teacher, Paul has been boldly instructing the Roman Christians in the fundamentals of the Christian faith. Now, in a more pastoral tone, he appeals to them to live what he has taught.

But the Romans are not asked to follow blindly what the apostle urges. There are good reasons, persuasive reasons for them to present their bodies as a living sacrifice to the Lord. Paul has been alluding to those reasons for eleven chapters. They are the mercies of God. The word "mercies" means compassion or longing. What are those mercies? They are every good thing God has done for His wayward people. They are all the compassions He has ever shown them. Every time we encounter the compassionate goodness of God in the first eleven chapters of Romans, that's God's mercies shown in action. Consider these.

The Mercies of God in Romans

- The gospel is the power of God unto salvation (1:16)
- The righteousness of God is revealed (1:17)
- God has given us the gift of eternal life (2:7)
- The Romans were justified freely through Christ Jesus (3:24)
- God is the God of Jews and Gentiles (3:29)
- Blessed are those whose lawless deeds are forgiven (4:7)
- Blessed is the one to whom God does not count sin (4:8)
- We have peace with God through our Lord Jesus Christ (5:1)
- Through Jesus Christ we have access to God the Father (5:2)
- We can rejoice in hope of the glory of God (5:2)
- We know that suffering ultimately produces hope (5:3-5)
- God's love has been poured into our hearts (5:5)

- We have the gift of God's Holy Spirit (5:5)
- While we were still sinners, Christ died for us (5:8)
- We have been justified by Christ's blood (5:9)
- We will be saved by Christ from the wrath of God (5:9)
- We were reconciled to God by the death of His Son (5:10)
- Jesus' obedience leads to our justification (5:19)
- We were buried with Christ in baptism (6:4)
- We have been set free from sin (6:22)
- We now receive the fruit that leads to sanctification (6:22)
- The gift of God is eternal life in Christ Jesus our Lord (6:23)
- There is now no condemnation for those in Christ (8:1)
- All who are led by the Spirit of God are sons of God (8:14)
- The Spirit Himself bears witness with our spirit (8:16)
- We are heirs of God and fellow heirs with Christ (8:17)
- For "the called", all things work together for good (8:28)
- Since God is for us, who can be against us (8:31)
- Nothing can separate us from the love of Christ (8:35)
- In all these things we are more than conquerors (8:37)
- Everyone who calls on the name of the Lord will be saved (10:13)
- The gifts and calling of God are irrevocable (11:29)
- From Him and through Him and to Him are all things (11:36)

I think we can all resonate with these mercies. We are all invited to present our lives in worshipful service to the Lord in gratitude for what He has already done for us. This is no *quid pro quo* arrangement; this is a thankful offering of our lives because of the sacrifice of Christ on our behalf. True spiritual formation is our grateful response to God's mercies, including our eternal salvation.

Present your bodies as a sacrifice

The command of this passage is simple: present your bodies as a sacrifice to God. But understanding and implementing that command is not so simple.

The word "present" in the language of Paul's day is the Greek word paristēmi. It means "to place beside or near, to put at one's disposal." Paul used the same word in Romans 6:13 when he wrote, "Do not present your members to sin as instruments for unrighteousness, but present yourselves to God as those who have been brought from death to life, and your members to God as instruments for righteousness."

80

The meaning of this word becomes clear when we remember that it is the same word used repeatedly for presenting sacrificial animals at the altar. Even if animals were not sacrificed, they were intentionally brought before the Lord to "present" the animal for God's exclusive use. The same was true for presenting children to the Lord. Luke 2:22, "And when the time came for their purification according to the Law of Moses, they [Joseph and Mary] brought him [Jesus] up to Jerusalem to present him to the Lord."

The word is also used in Colossians 1:22 of the cleansing power of Jesus' blood to make us acceptable to God: "He has now reconciled in his body of flesh by his death, in order to present you holy and blameless and above reproach before him." And later in this same chapter, verse 28, the word is used as the *raison d'etre* for spiritual formation: "Him we proclaim, warning everyone and teaching everyone with all wisdom, that we may present everyone mature in Christ."

To present our bodies, therefore, is a matter of stepping up before God, laying down our life on the altar of gratitude, and saying to Him, "Here, Lord. Take it. It's yours." It's the offer a slave makes to his kind master, a lump of clay makes to the skillful potter, or debtor makes to his forgiving creditor. (On the further use of this word see also: Acts 1:3; 9:41; 23:33; Romans 6:13, 16, 19; and 2 Corinthians 4:14).

That Paul chose to use this word "present" both here and in Chapter 6 was not coincidental. He intended to contrast the two options believers have regarding their behavior: They can either present themselves to sin, (that is, make themselves available to sin to fulfill its purposes), or they can present themselves to God, (that is, make themselves available for His use to fulfill His purposes). Since we naturally choose to serve sin, the transformation in our lives comes when we get our minds to willfully choose to serve the Savior.

Here the apostle puts his finger on the real pulse of spiritual formation. It's not so much what we do while we sit quietly and wait for God, but what we do after we leave the silence and solitude and re-enter the messed-up world that awaits us. If that quiet time with God, that moment of personal intimacy, does not translate into a lifestyle that demonstrates our love and respect for God on an on-going basis, our island of quiet has not been transformational. It simply has become a place to get away, not a springboard for service.

Presenting both body and mind

In a correct study of the passage, we should not rigidly separate the "body" of verse 1 and the "mind" of verse 2. To do so would be akin to the dualism that was so prevalent in Greek philosophy. Paul views human beings holistically, and thus he sees an intimate connection between what we think and what we do. So while the language of animal sacrifice is used here, the idea is not simply that we would give up our bodies to the Lord, but rather that we would render our whole being to Him. That, in itself, is a transformation for most people. John Calvin explained it this way: "By bodies he means not only our skin and bones but the totality of which we are composed. He adopted this word that he might more fully designate all that we are, for the members of the body are the instruments by which we carry out our purposes."[19]

The allusion to chapter 6 also aids our understanding of what Paul meant by "your bodies" in 12:1–2. In Romans 6:12–13 the apostle used the Greek words *soma* ("body") and *melos* ("member") almost interchangeably. To offer for the Lord's service our bodies is also to offer our minds, our eyes, our ears, our hands, our feet, our feelings, and our energies. When we offer our bodies, we offer the complete package, everything we are or ever will be, and everything we have or ever will have. So we must be careful when we say to the Lord, "Here am I! Send me" (Isaiah 6:8), for we are laying on the altar of gratitude our bodies, minds, goals, bank accounts, days, and years. We are offering to God everything.

Paul calls this offering a "sacrifice" (Greek: *thusia*). We are giving up any claim to ourselves. This sacrifice is a genuine commitment to God that embraces every area of our lives. It is described with three adjectives:

- living
- holy
- acceptable

English Bible scholar C. E. B. Cranfield correctly notes that many English readers gain a wrong impression of the text since some English versions translate the phrase "living sacrifice, holy and well pleasing to God," which suggests that "living sacrifice" is somehow separable from the adjectives "holy" and "well pleasing" in the Greek text. In fact, all three adjectives ("living," "holy," and "well pleasing") follow θυσίαν, and thus there is no exegetical warrant for isolating the word "living".[20]

Any sacrifice that does not exhibit these three character qualities is unacceptable to God. That's serious, so we'd better take a closer look at these three important adjectives.

1. A living sacrifice

The sacrifice offered by the saint in the New Testament is different from the sacrifice offered by the saint in the Old Testament. The great people of faith in the Old Testament (Moses, Abraham, Rachel, David, etc.) offered a live animal, but the intent of the sacrifice was to kill it. It was the loss of life that was the sacrifice, not the animal itself.

Today God may not necessarily be calling us to lose our lives, but *to give to Him* what constitutes our lives. The sacrifice is not giving *up*, it is giving *to*. Hence the emphasis in Romans 6 of yielding our members, all we are, to God. We are giving our lives and everything that makes up our lives *to* God for His use. We don't give Him our death; we give Him our life, not to be killed but to be lived.

2. A holy sacrifice

The Greek word *agios* (usually translated "holy") describes two related concepts. In the first, it describes being set apart for God's service specifically within the sacrificial system. But in order to be set apart, the object had to meet a high standard, so *agios* can also be related to the concept of being "pure" or "perfect". Perhaps Paul has both meanings in view here.

> *"A holy sacrifice is when we give ourselves to God as a pure, sanctified vessel, fit for His use."*

A holy sacrifice is both set apart to God for use as a sacrifice and it is pure, undefiled, presenting itself without guile or hidden agenda. This is likely the intent of the solemn command in Scripture, "Consecrate yourselves, therefore, and be holy; for I am the LORD your God. Keep my statutes and do them; I am the LORD who sanctifies you" (Leviticus 20:7-8; see also: 1 Peter 1:15-16).

To be a "holy" sacrifice means to be the product of the sanctifying influence of the Holy Spirit on our lives. When we "walk by the Spirit" we will not "gratify the desires of the flesh" because "the desires of the flesh are against the Spirit, and the desires of the Spirit are against the flesh, for these are opposed to each other" (Galatians 5:16-17).

So, here again, is the choice you face: to "present" yourself (your members—mind, heart, body, etc.) to sin as an instrument for unrighteousness, or to "present yourselves to God as those who have been brought from death to life, and your members to God as instruments for righteousness" (Romans 6:13). A holy sacrifice is not a sinless sacrifice—one without spot or blemish. Only Jesus could provide that. A holy sacrifice is when we give ourselves to God as a pure, sanctified vessel, fit for His use.

3. An acceptable sacrifice

The third qualifier every sacrifice must demonstrate is acceptability. The word "acceptable" (Greek: *euarestos*) means well pleasing, that which affords pleasure or a sense of satisfaction to others." Perhaps the best way to understand the meaning of the word is through its use elsewhere in the New Testament. Consider these examples.

- "Whoever thus serves Christ is *acceptable* to God and approved by men" (Romans 14:18).
- "So whether we are at home or away, we make it our aim to *please* him [Christ]" (2 Corinthians 5:9).
- "Walk as children of light (for the fruit of light is found in all that is good and right and true), and try to discern what is *pleasing* to the Lord" (Ephesians 5:8-10).
- "I am well supplied, having received from Epaphroditus the gifts you sent, a fragrant offering, a sacrifice acceptable and *pleasing* to God" (Philippians 4:18).
- "Children, obey your parents in everything, for this *pleases* the Lord" (Colossians 3:20).
- "Now may the God of peace who brought again from the dead our Lord Jesus . . . equip you with everything good that you may do his will, working in us, that which is *pleasing* in his sight, through Jesus Christ . . ." (Hebrews 13:20-21).

Only a sacrifice which presents to God a holy life pleases the Father. We can give Him our gold, our time, or our silence. But if we really want to enjoy our Heavenly Father's acceptance, we are invited to give Him ourselves. This is the kind of sacrifice that is not only acceptable to God, but is most heartily welcomed by Him.

Doing the logical thing

When I was growing up my family lived in a large country home that my father and mother had built with their own hands. Unfortunately, they never finished the second level of the house until I went off to college and they no longer needed it. My older brother and I shared a room on the first floor, across the hall from our parent's bedroom.

I remember when I was about 8, my older brother being 10, receiving the scare of my life. Our unfinished upstairs was a threatening place at night. There were unlit dormers up there surely filled with monsters lurking to devour an 8-year-old. In fact, there was only one light bulb hanging from the ceiling to light the entire floor. And speaking of floor, there was none—no flooring, that is. When you walked from one end of the upstairs to the other you had carefully walk only on the joist.

One night my mother asked my brother and me to go up into that potential graveyard and fetch a kitchen broom that she had left up there during the day. Apparently she thought we were expendable; my father and she were still young; they could have more children. So in great fear and trepidation we flipped on the light switch at the bottom of the stairs and made our way up and all the way to the other end of the house where the broom was. It's important to remember that when you flip that one switch, you turn on the power to everything electrical up there, including our old radio.

For those of you born in recent decades, before we had iPods and iPhones, radios had tubes in them that had to warm up before any sound came out. Well, as we made our way across the joist to the broom, about sixty seconds later the tubes in that old radio warmed up. The CBS Mystery Theater was on, and just as my brother and I reached for the broom in that distant, dimly lit corner, a sinister voice came from the radio that said, "You touch that and you're a dead man."

I don't know how many joists our little feet hit as we sped across the upstairs and down the steps, but it couldn't have been many.

There was only one reason why we left in such a hurry. Instinct. It was the adrenalin of human instant that carried us terrified to the safety below. But that instinct was both emotional and rational. Getting out of there was the emotional thing to do—we were scared out of our wits. It was also the rational thing to do—we could be eaten by who knows what after we were shot. One instinct—two sources.

That's true of the last part of Romans 12:1 as well. When describing the sacrifice of ourselves to God, the apostle says this is "your spiritual worship." The adjectival modifier, either translated "reasonable" or "spiritual," is from the Greek word *logikos* and is an extremely rare word. This verse is the only place Paul uses it, and the only other place it occurs in the New Testament is in 1 Peter 2:2.

While both usages may be true, like my emotional and rational reasons for fleeing our dark upstairs, it is important to determine exactly which meaning Paul had in mind when he wrote that the sacrifice of our selves is both spiritual and rational. At first glance, these words sound like complete opposites.

The word reminds us of our English word *logical*. But the meaning of a word is not determined first by its etymology, but by its use in a given context. In many newer versions and paraphrases of the Bible (NIV, NASB, ESV, HCSG, TNIV) the translators have opted to go with the understanding of "spiritual." Paul would then be arguing that to give ourselves as a sacrifice to God is the spiritual thing to do because it is the ultimate act of worship.

Other versions (CEV, Young's Literal Translation, KJV, Wycliffe New Testament, NKJV, etc.) have opted for the concept of rationality. (It appears as if the Amplified Bible covered both bases with their paraphrase: "which is your reasonable [rational, intelligent] service and spiritual worship.")

If we are to understand this phrase as "spiritual worship," the apostle is saying that the spiritual service of worship encompasses everything in the believer's life. Nothing is left out. Everything we do and say, everything we have, everything we are, is now sanctified as an offering and appropriately considered "worship."

That's huge. The ramifications of that are immense. There is no part of our lives as Christ-followers which is too small or insignificant to be sanctified to the Lord and given to him as an act of worship. In many ways this is a primary emphasis of spiritual formation: to help us live the entirety of life as worship to God. Attitudes, actions, habits, the things we do, the way we feel—all are to be sanctified before the Lord and transformed from gifts to the world into gifts to God. That's our worship.

Logical over Spiritual

But what does Paul have in mind in Romans 12:1? While the concept of spiritual worship is an accurate possibility, I believe the concept of reasonable service is the better option. Here's why.

First, there's the grammar. The classic *A Greek-English Lexicon of the New Testament and Other Early Christian Literature*, based on Walter Bauer's *Griechish-Deutsches Worterbuch*, revised and edited by Frederick William Danker, defines the Greek word *logikos* as "being carefully thought through."[21]

A Lexicon Abridged from Liddell and Scott's Greek-English Lexicon authored by Henry George Liddel, Robert Scott and James Morris Whiton lists a number of meanings, the most appropriate of which for this context is "possessed of reason, intellectual."[22] And while we do not determine the meaning of a word simply by its etymology, it seems the grammar clearly favors the understanding of logical or rational.

But if context, the way a word is used, is a better determiner of what a word means, we must consider the context of Romans 12:1. Paul has been enumerating the "mercies" of God in the first eleven chapters, as we've already shown. They have all been doctrinal in nature. Here the apostle initiates the practical conclusions that are normal in his letters. It's time to connect the dots, to take theology and turn it into life. Paul even uses the connective word "therefore" in linking the two.

In light of all that God has done for us, in view of all His mercies, based on the normative response to a God who "shows his love for us in that while we were still sinners, Christ died for us" (Romans 5:8), what is our reasonable response to that love? What is the rational thing for a sinner to do who has been bathed in the blood of Jesus and baptized into God's righteousness without having met any pre-conditions? Paul's answer is Romans 12:1.

A rational response to undeserved mercies

Considering its position in the sixteen chapters of Paul's Epistle to the Romans, if nothing else, Romans 12:1-2 is certainly telling us that a right and proper response—hence the logical, reasonable and rational response—to the mercies God has showered upon us is to offer ourselves wholeheartedly to Him as sacrifices, living, holy, and well-pleasing. It's the idea that Isaac Watts' great hymn communicates so poetically: "Love so amazing, so divine, demands my heart, my life, my all."

Thus, spiritual formation is not just about what we learn; it's about what we do with what we learn. It's about transformation not just information. Since much of Paul's Epistle to the Romans is instruction (it is the most doctrinal book he wrote), and since Paul's *modus operandi* is to wait until after instruction to begin application, it is here—Romans 12:1-2—that the apostle begins to show us the transformation in lifestyle that must always accompany instruction in the eternal Word of God.

If we are to deepen our relationship with God, if we are to grow spiritually, if we are to make any progress down the road toward spiritual maturity, it will require a transformation in how we see ourselves before God. We are not paupers, hermits, mystics or monks. We are servants presenting everything we are and everything we have to God for worshipful service as the logical consequence of receiving His undeserved mercies.

> *"Let's be honest. We do not live in an environment that is conducive to being intimate with God, knocking off the rough edges of our spirituality, or making much progress down the road to spiritual maturity."*

But note that it's one thing to challenge someone with a goal and encourage them to try and reach it; and it's entirely something else to show that person how to reach that goal. Here the apostle does not fail. In Romans 12:2 Paul gets deeper into why these two verses are so crucial to our understanding of spiritual formation. In verse 2 the apostle shows us both what we should do and not do in order to become more like God. Here's how to become more intimate with God and get cracking on the road to spiritual maturity. This is what the Bible says.

The pledge for non-conformity

In verse 1 Paul exhorted his readers to present their bodies as sacrifices to God. In verse 2 he switches to the imperative mood to more directly influence his readers. The two imperatives, "be conformed" (Greek: *syschēmatizesthe)* and "be transformed" (Greek: *metamorphousthe)* are both present tense and barely pronounceable. They are things we do on an on-going basis. They are the things we do in life, on a date, at the office, not at a spiritual retreat or in the Sunday service. They are the opposite sides of the same coin, the continuing battle both to evade that which keeps us from God and to enhance that which helps us be more intimate with Him.

First, the negative. "Do not be conformed to this world." The verb means "to form according to a pattern." It refers to when someone assumes an outward expression that does not come from within, an appearance that is not representative of what we are down deep inside.

Let's be honest. We do not live in an environment which is conducive to being intimate with God, knocking off the rough edges of our spirituality, or making much progress down the road toward spiritual maturity. Quite the opposite. We live in a world where friends, television, the Internet, magazines, video games, images, clubs, our insatiable desire to spend, and a whole lot more often have a debilitating influence on our spirituality and the spirituality of those we love. When it comes to fostering an intimate relationship with God, this world just isn't a very helpful place.

The "world" (literally *age*), as Paul uses it here, means the society or system that man has built in order to make himself happy without God. It is the human kingdom, a kingdom antagonistic to God. In the kingdom of the world people think they are in control, but really Satan is the prince of this kingdom (2 Corinthians 4:4; John 12:31; 14:30; 16:11). Satan already has us—we are born into his kingdom, but he keeps us in bondage through the lust of the eyes, the lust of the flesh, and the pride of life (1 John 2:16 NKJV). Once he gets us, he intends to keep us. The kingdom of this age has its own music, religion, amusements, places to hang out, politics, culture and customs.

We often "wear" this kingdom on the outside. You see it in our iPhones, faces, clothes, attitudes, choices, associates, thoughts and actions. We adopt a worldview that is more influenced by today's media than the Word of God. We are touched by causes that tug at our heart, even if they run counter to our Christian faith. We begin to adapt to the world rather than impact it. But the real problem is seepage. What we wear on the outside often seeps into our heart and mind and begins to poison us internally.

Our personal spiritual formation is often stalled because of conformity to the world. When we disregard God and His Word, when we substitute biblical spirituality with non-biblical rituals, when we look to the mysticism and morality of this age instead of breadth and depth of the power of the Holy Spirit within us, we make little or no progress toward spiritual maturity. We may feel spiritual, but we aren't godly. Transformation is happening, but it's going the wrong way. We are being transformed into the comfort of the kingdom of this world.

Romans 12:1 is the apostle's plea for a pledge of non-conformity. It's a plea not to become play dough to the world's forms and shapes. Spiritual transformation cannot occur in an environment in which we are losing ground to the kingdom of this world.

The pledge for new thinking

That's why there is a positive side to this coin. Paul now has something positive to say about spiritual transformation. "But be transformed by the renewal of your mind" (v. 2). This imperative has great and lasting bearing on our discussion of spiritual formation.

While much being written today about spiritual formation is tainted with the mystical, the esoteric, even the ritualistic, Paul's approach is much more down to earth. For the apostle, spiritual formation is not just a matter of the heart (or even primarily a matter of the heart); it is a matter of the mind. Don't forget what we already said about presenting ourselves holistically to God—everything we are and everything we have. When we present our bodies as a sacrifice to God, we present our heart, our mind, our will, our attitudes, our everything.

Please don't miss this. The Bible regards the mind, not the spiritual disciplines, as the key to spiritual transformation. The way to keep from being squeezed into the world's mold is by the renewal of the mind. The road that leads to deeper spirituality runs through the mind. We don't become more intimate with God when we empty our mind; we become more intimate with Him when we fill it with His Word. Getting to know God doesn't mean sitting in silence, stripping away the outer layers of the self to find God at our center. It means filling our mind with the things of God so we can know Him better. That was Paul's desire: "that I may know him . . ." (Philippians 3:10).

Now here's something to think about. Will we get to know God better by walking solemnly through a labyrinth or by spending quality time with Him in His Word? Will we discover God through the discipline of emptying our minds or through the discipline of engaging His Word with our minds? Will we more likely meet God in the stillness of the moment listening for an inaudible voice or through what He has already said to us about Himself that has been written down by holy men who were guided to write by God's Spirit?

Don't sidestep these questions. They demand honest answers.

Our invitation is to examine carefully what the apostle says here. In Romans 12:2 Paul employs the Greek verb *metamorphoo*: "be transformed by the renewal of your mind." This verb occurs only four times in the New Testament. In Matthew 17:2 and Mark 9:2 it refers to Jesus' transfiguration and is talking about a *physical* transformation. Jesus was transformed in His appearance before the disciples. Peter, James and John saw the glorious essence of who Jesus is.

But Paul is not talking about a physical transformation. He is talking about the transformation of the mind, a change in the way we think, a change in the way we view the world around us, a change in how we see God's truth as recorded in His Word as opposed to the truth that originates in the mind of man.

What is needed is transformation on the inside, inner change, the transformation of our inner disposition. But Paul understands that such a change must run through the highway of the mind. There is no change in the heart, no change in our inner being, that does not begin with a transformation of the mind—what Paul calls the renewal of the mind.

The word *nous* in Greek, translated as "mind" here, is almost exclusively a Pauline word in the New Testament. Paul uses it specifically to describe our mental faculties, but he also uses it more generally to refer to the entire state of our mental and moral being. Paul's desire is that, as followers of Christ, we would think differently, think about different things (Philippians 4:8) from what our friends and family who are not followers of Christ think.

Logical questions

If the call not to be conformed to this world is a plea for a pledge of non-conformity, the call to the renewal of our minds must be a pledge of conformity—conformity to the thinking of God. So let me ask you again: Where will you most likely encounter the thinking of God? Where are you most apt to discover what's on God's mind and in His heart? Where has God revealed His mind to you? What book would you suspect to be the most helpful in discovering the will of God, the way of God, and the wisdom of God?

Maybe reading God's Word is a better approach to becoming like God, feeling God's heart, and knowing His mind. Think about it honestly and take the pledge—the pledge for non-conformity to the way the world approaches spiritual formation and the pledge for conformity to the way God's Word describes it.

CHAPTER 8

The 3 "R"s of Bible Engagement

There it sits.
On the coffee table. Maybe stuck on a high shelf. Perhaps neatly tucked away in the drawer by the bed. Most North Americans know it's somewhere in the room, but so rarely reads the Bible that they can't immediately put their hands on it.

It's paradoxical—on one hand, incredible things are happening today in the fields of Bible publishing and distribution. Consider:

- The Palestine Bible Society recently conducted a "Proclaim It" Scripture encounter media blitz that exposed as many as 10,000 Palestinians to the Word of God.
- Just two years ago the Bible Society of Brazil distributed 6 million Bibles, surpassing its goal of 5.7 million. According to the World Christian Database,[23] approximately 83 million Bibles are distributed globally per year.
- The Gideons International started distributing the Word of God in 1908. Today the organization has more than 290,000 members and since 1908 they have distributed more than 1.6 billion Bibles and New Testaments around the world, 79.8 million copies just last year. The Gideons claim that, on average, more than two copies of God's Word are distributed every second; over one million Bibles and New Testaments are distributed every 4.5 days.[24]

Why is the Bible the best-selling, least-read book of all time? The problem does not lie with the Bible Societies or the Gideons. I thank God for them. I have worked closely with the good folks at the Gideons International. But before we get too giddy about these unparalleled distribution statistics, consider one of the foundational themes of this book: an unopened Bible is no better than no Bible at all. The problem today does not lie with publication or distribution, the problem lies with us.

But we can do something about it.

The key lies with *engagement.* We must open the Bible and read it like our lives depended on it. And a practical solution is much closer than you may think.

Choices, choices

It's not that we lack choices in which Bible to read. We have more choices than we can handle. Each year I await the arrival of my Bible catalogue from Christianbook.com. Over the years I have purchased many Bibles from them. As I write this, the latest Bible catalog came the day before yesterday. In that Christian Book Distributers catalog there were no less than 2,984 different kinds, sizes, and colors of Bibles to choose from. (Yes, I counted them). That's an increase of 926 possible Bible purchases over their catalog just five years ago.

Today, you can buy Bibles with red covers, blue covers, brown covers, black covers, burgundy covers—even hydrangea blue, plum, and toffee-colored covers.

You can buy hardcover, imitation leather, bonded leather, genuine leather, and water buffalo calfskin.

You can purchase our favorite translation: the NCV, HSCB, NAB, CEV, NCV, RSV, NRSV, NEB, ESV, NLT and more.

You can buy the ASV of 1901 or the revision of that, the NASB of 1971. There's even an NASB updated version of 1995.

If you are getting tired of your NIV there's the TNIV or the UK NIV.

Of course there's always the good old King James Version, but if you want an updated version of this classic there's the NKJV and even the 21st Century KJV.

If you don't like all the initials there are also the Wycliffe New Testament, the Amplified version, God's Word, The Message or The Message, Remix 2.0.

And then there are age- or life-appropriate Bibles—the Couples Bible, the Seniors Bible, Children's Bibles, the Veggie Tales Bible, the Bug Collection Bible, the Early Reader's Bible, The Story for Teens and the New Believer's Bible.

And what about the specialty Bibles: there's the Apologetics Bible, the In Touch Ministries Bible, the Maxwell Leadership Bible the NIV Stewardship Study Bible, the God's Precious Promises Bible, the Pursuit of God Bible, the Livin' Out Your Faith Bible, the Charles Stanley Life Principles Bible, the KJV Reese Chronological Bible, the Oswald Chambers Devotional Bible, and more.

Hold on. I haven't even mentioned the reference Bibles. There's: the ESV Classic Reference Bible, the ESV Personal-Size Reference Bible the NLT Slimline Reference Bible, the NIV Thinline Reference Bible, the Nelson NKJV Classic Giant-Print Center-Column Reference Bible, the NASB Compact Reference Bible, the NIV Compact Thinline Reference Bible, the KJV Giant-Print Personal-Size Reference Bible, the KJV Super Giant-Print Reference Bible and others.

Still more choices

Had enough? I'll quit, but wait, not just yet because I haven't said anything about those study Bibles. Choose from the Dake Study Bible, the ESV Study Bible, the Fire Bible, the Life Application Study Bible, the Life in the Spirit Study Bible, the MacArthur Study Bible, the Archaeological Study Bible, The Case for Christ Study Bible, the Quest Study Bible, the New Spirit-Filled Life Bible, the NOT Transformation Study Bible. The Ryrie Study Bible, the Scofield Study Bible, the Thompson Chain-Reference Study Bible, the Jeremiah Study Bible, the Zondervan Study Bible, and the New Inductive Study Bible.

Oh, and did I fail to mention these are only Bibles in the English language?

Okay, now I'll quit. I purposely belabored the point to illustrate again the root problem in the Evangelical world today.

The problem is not that we don't have a Bible.

The problem is we don't read the one we have.

That's why the new Christian spirituality movement is gaining so much traction in the Church today, but biblical understanding and changed lives are not following.

> *"The Bible is the best-selling, least-read book of all time."*

We all want our time spent with God to be meaningful, not mindless. We want to take Christ's yoke on us and learn of Him. This book consistently argues that biblical spirituality is being hijacked, that even the Christian has marginalized the Bible in the pursuit of personal spirituality.

So, let's get down to brass tacks. How do we meaningfully engage God's Word? Throughout this book I have spoken of Bible engagement as more than reading and checking off a reading guide. Bible engagement is the practice of consistently receiving God's Word, thoughtfully reflecting on what you have read or heard, and obediently responding with a positive, biblical lifestyle. Now I want to be more specific about how Bible engagement works. Let's talk about the three "R"s of Bible engagement. When I talk about our need to remember the three "R"s, I'm not talking about a magical formula, a monastic practice, or a mystical equation.

I'm talking about three things the Bible says we must do if we are to make any measurable progress toward spiritual maturity. Could there be more than the three "R"s? Certainly, but like vitamins, these are the minimum daily requirement. Here they are—the three "R"s.

#1. RECEIVE

Today when we talk about receiving the Word of God we must include all the methods that modern technology has placed at our disposal. Most of us still read our Bible. We may do it from that book we love with a leather cover. Or we can receive the text of Scripture on our Blackberry, iPad, cell phone, e-reader or similar hand-held device. For some who are illiterate or may have difficulty seeing, receiving God's Word could mean hearing it read on a CD or DVD. But most of us will still receive the Bible by reading it. So, for all intents and purposes, when we say "receive" we most frequently mean "read."

To grow spiritually we must take the initiative to open our Bibles and begin to read them. This sounds so simple, but this first step is the one where the enemy so very often halts our progress. Reading is fundamental, but it's not an end in itself. It is only step one. But we can't take step two until we take step one.

A young king's example

When eight-year-old Josiah began to reign in Judah, he wanted to please the Lord, so at age 20 he instituted religious reforms among God's people. In the process of restoring the temple, when Josiah was only 26, an important discovery was made. 2 Chronicles 34:14-19 says:

"Hilkiah the priest found the Book of the Law of the LORD given through Moses. Then Hilkiah answered and said to Shaphan the secretary, 'I have found the Book of the Law in the house of the LORD.' And Hilkiah gave the book to Shaphan. Shaphan brought the book to the king . . . Then Shaphan the secretary told the king, 'Hilkiah the priest has given me a book.'"

Shaphan then read from the Book of the Law before the king. And when the king heard the words of the Law, he tore his clothes. Do you see the very simple truth illustrated here? God's Word was opened and *read*. You can't start anywhere else. Example after example in Scripture shows this truth. Read the Book.

A cupbearer's example

More than 175 years later Nehemiah returned to the Holy City to rebuild the rubble of Jerusalem's walls. When they finished, in celebration everyone gathered at the Water Gate and Nehemiah 8:2-3, 8 tells what happened.

"Ezra the priest brought the Law before the assembly, both men and women and all who could understand what they heard, on the first day of the seventh month. And he read from it facing the square before the Water Gate from early morning until midday, in the presence of the men and the women and those who could understand. And the ears of all the people were attentive to the Book of the Law. . . They read from the book, from the Law of God, clearly, and they gave the sense, so that the people understood the reading."

From early morning until midday, everyone stood in the hot sun and attentively listened as the Law of God was *read*. Read the Book.

Nehemiah 9 shows a similar practice. "And they stood up in their place and read from the Book of the Law of the Lord their God for a quarter of the day" (v. 3). Read the Book.

As does Nehemiah 13:1, "On that day they read from the Book of Moses in the hearing of the people." Read the Book.

An old prophet's example

When God was revealing His mind to His prophet Jeremiah, the prophet was banned from entering the house of the LORD so he told his scribe Baruch,

"You are to go, and on a day of fasting in the hearing of all the people in the LORD's house you shall read the words of the LORD from the scroll that you have written at my dictation. You shall read them also in the hearing of all the men of Judah. . . And Baruch the son of Neriah did all that Jeremiah the prophet ordered him about reading from the scroll the words of the LORD in the LORD's house." Jeremiah 36:6-8

A year later, "in the hearing of all the people, Baruch read the words of Jeremiah from the scroll in the house of the LORD" (v. 10). Read the Book.

Jesus' example

Let's jump to the New Testament. God expects His people to read His Word. Copies of the Bible are not copied or printed to be kept in a Torah ark, (Hebrew: *Aron Kodesh*) or cabinet on the eastern wall of the synagogue. Nor should our Bible be sitting idly on a shelf, in the back of a pew or on our coffee table. Think how often Jesus said to the Jews of his day, "Have you not read . . . " (see Matthew 12:3-5; 19:4; 21:16, 42; 22:31; Mark 2:25; 12:10, 26; Luke 6:3). God expects us to read His Word, not just selected, favorite portions, but the whole thing. Read the Book.

Likewise, it was the custom of the Savior to enter a synagogue and read the Hebrew Scriptures (Luke 4:16). When the New Testament God-inspired letters were circulated among the churches, Paul expected them to be read, and so did God (Colossians 4:16). "I put you under oath before the Lord to have this letter read to all the brothers" (1 Thessalonians 5:27). Read the Book.

The first step in the practice of engaging Scripture is very simply reading—not speed reading or spot reading, but reading with reverence and understanding. We can never accomplish anything more with God's Word until we begin to read it.

Reading for God's agenda

In addition, we must read for God's agenda, not for our own. This is something many people have never thought about. Perhaps transformation never happens when we read our Bibles because we have forgotten the number of personal pronouns in God's promise of Isaiah 55:11, "So shall my word be that goes out from my mouth; it shall not return to me empty, but it shall accomplish that which I purpose, and shall succeed in the thing for which I sent it." We come to the Bible looking for answers, looking for promises, looking for comfort, looking for direction. But with each of these "looks" we are looking for what the Bible can do for *us*. We bring our agenda to reading the Bible and we are disappointed when our agenda isn't realized. Isaiah 55:11 indicates the Bible is about God, not about you.

The next time you read your Bible, I encourage you to set aside every expectation you bring to your reading. Don't look for the biblical text to flatter, inspire, please, or even interest you. That's one of Satan's weapons on the spiritual battlefield. Instead, read the text to meet God there and let Him reveal Himself and His agenda to you. His agenda will transform you.

Reading the Bible once with God's agenda is good for you, but once is not enough. Bible engagement must become a habit; statistics say at least a four-time-per-week habit. We need to read the Word of God and rehearse it in our minds, but we will greatly benefit from reading it again. That leads me to the second of the three "R"s.

#2. REFLECT

Three words emerge when I think of rehearsing something again and again— meditate, metabolize, and memorize. All three are necessary if we are to make progress on the road to spiritual maturity.

> *"While some advocate a kind of meditation in which you do your best to empty your mind, Christian meditation always involves filling your mind with God and His truth."*

In his book, *Mere Christianity*, C. S. Lewis argues that once we've decided to believe in something (based on the evidence *for* it) we must be reminded of that evidence regularly. No belief, Lewis says, will "automatically remain alive in the mind" without being fed.[25] This is why reflecting on what you read over and over in your mind is so important.

Treasuring thoughts in our hearts

True meditation means we mull something over in our minds. We continually ponder the things that we learn from reading the Bible. This is what Mary did when the baby Jesus was born. She "treasured up all these things, pondering them in her heart" (Luke 2:19). Mary's "heart" is not the organ that pumps blood but the seat of her soul or mind, the fountain of her thoughts, passions, desires, appetites, affections, etc. She went over the events that had just taken place again and again in her mind. That's reflection. We need to do that with what we read in God's Word.

In the Hebrew Old Testament the word used for this reflection is *suwm*. Here are some of the verses where you find that word used.

- Exodus 17:14, "Then the LORD said to Moses, Write this as a memorial in a book, and *recite* it in the ears of Joshua, that I will utterly blot out the memory of Amalek from under heaven." The word is "recite."

- Nehemiah 8:8, "They read from the book, from the Law of God, clearly, and they *gave the sense*, so that the people understood the reading."
- Job 1:8, "And the LORD said to Satan, 'Have you *considered* my servant Job, that there is none like him on the earth, a blameless and upright man, who fears God and turns away from evil?" The word "considered" is repeated in Job 2:3

Additionally, the New Testament uses a variety of Greek words for the concept of rehearsing something in the mind and reflecting on it. Consider two examples.

- In the story of Philip and the Ethiopian, Acts 8:28-30 says the eunuch "was reading the prophet Isaiah. . . So Philip ran to him and heard him reading Isaiah the prophet and asked, 'Do you understand what you are reading?'" This last phrase uses the Greek *anaginosko* meaning "to distinguish between," or "to recognize." It suggests cogitation, rehearsal in the mind, meditation.
- The word appears in Acts 13:27 referring to those who live in Jerusalem who "did not *recognize* him [Jesus] nor understand the utterances of the prophets, which are read every Sabbath, fulfilled them by condemning him." Also Acts 15:21: "For from ancient generations Moses has had in every city those who proclaim him, for he is *read* every Sabbath in the synagogues."

Each of these passages indicate that the Scriptures were read every Sabbath, but apparently those who read them never thought much about them until the next Sabbath (see 2 Corinthians 3:12-18). This sounds a bit like church today, doesn't it? We remember to read (at least in church) but we fail to remember the second "R"—to reflect on what we have read in God's Word.

Metabolizing the Word

Reflecting on the Word means both *meditating* on it and *metabolizing* it. When it comes to Bible reading, you should not just read it, check it off your reading guide, and feel good about yourself. We all must assimilate what we have read into our spiritual metabolic being. The Word becomes a part of us, it provides the energy for our journey toward spiritual maturity.

Until we have read and assimilated God's Word into our lives, we have not engaged in a process of change. I encourage Christians everywhere to metabolize the Word of God. Make it a part of the "warp and woof" of your being. Make it so much a part of who you are that you bleed Bible, you think in terms of Bible, you act Bible. When people see you, let them see the evidence of God's Word metabolized in you.

But there is another important aspect to reflecting on the Bible. It's retaining what we have meditated on and metabolized. The key to retention is memorizing the Word.

Memorizing the Word

When I was a boy I remember preachers and evangelists coming to our church and telling stories about prisoners of war during World War II. They were locked up in Nazi prison camps without a Bible and with no spiritual mentors to encourage them. All they had were their minds and those portions of God's Word they had memorized. That's what sustained them.

I thought, "Cool." But while I've visited Dachau, Buchenwald, Auschwitz, and several other Nazi prison camps, I've never been incarcerated in one. God willing, I never will be. So what's the benefit to my spiritual life if I memorize Scripture? The answer is "Plenty."

- **Memorization aids retention.** Memorizing God's Word puts it at our fingertips in the most colossal computer every created—our human brain. It's there when we need it.
- **Memorization places the *defensive* power of the Holy Spirit at our disposal.** When Scripture is stored in our minds, it is available for the Holy Spirit to bring to our attention and remind us of God's truth just when we need it most. Nobody knew better the validity of storing up Scripture than the Lord Jesus Himself. Tempted by Satan in the hot and lonely wilderness of Judea, Jesus proved this principle (Matthew 4:1-11), and answered Satan with Scripture.
- **Memorization places the *offensive* power of the Holy Spirit at our disposal.** Just as memorizing Scripture becomes the tool the Holy Spirit uses to ward off the attacks of the evil one, memorizing Scripture becomes the tool the He uses to gain yardage as you move down the field toward your goal of spiritual maturity.

If you saw the 2010 film "The Book of Eli" starring Denzel Washington, you have a vivid reminder of the importance of memorizing Scripture. Memorizing the Bible not only keeps your mind healthy as you age physically, it helps you to know what's on God's mind as you mature spiritually.

Now, for the third of the three "R"s.

#3. RESPOND

Spiritual formation is not formation in theory. It is formation in life. So retaining Scripture in our minds is of little use until we live it out in our lives. We have to respond to what we tuck away in our heads. It's living the "foot life" that James talks about.

Biblical meditation must always lead to application. This is where the lonely monks in monasteries went wrong. They sought to get close to the Lord by withdrawing from the world completely. The Bible always counsels us to overcome the world, not retreat from it.

For instance, God's Word says, "He who is in you is greater than he who is in the world. They are from the world; therefore they speak from the world, and the world listens to them" (I John 4:4-5).

And Jesus warned His disciples "If you were of the world, the world would love you as its own; but because you are not of the world, but I chose you out of the world, therefore the world hates you" (John 15:19).

The Apostle John's tiny epistles are similarly rooted in promoting the concept of living what we believe. "By this we know love, that he laid down his life for us, and we ought to lay down our lives for the brothers. But if anyone has the world's goods and sees his brother in need, yet closes his heart against him, how does God's love abide in him? Little children, let us not love in word or talk but in deed and in truth" (1 John 3:16-18).

The Apostle James agrees. "Therefore put away all filthiness and rampant wickedness and receive with meekness the implanted word, which is able to save your souls. But be doers of the word, and not hearers only, deceiving yourselves" (James 1:21-22).

God's secret for success

Perhaps the greatest call in the Bible to meditate, metabolize and memorize the Word of God is found in Joshua 1:8. But while we tend to focus on the meditating half of the verse, God instructed Joshua what he must do with his meditation. "This Book of the Law shall not depart from your mouth, but you shall meditate on it day and night, *so that you may be careful to do according to all that is written in it.* For then you will make your way prosperous, and then you will have good success" [*italics* mine]. The promise of prosperous ways and good success do not come as a result of meditation alone; they come as a result of being careful *to do* all we have meditated on, memorized, and metabolized into our spiritual system.

Spiritual formation never happens if we don't insist that Scriptural meditation must lead to Scriptural application.

Similarly, I always encourage people to read "through" the Bible to reach the Author. In other words, read "through" the stories, the battles, the doctrine and the history to find the Author Himself, feel the heart of God, and know the mind of God.

> *"When we see the Bible as a means to a dynamic relationship with God, we can't get enough of it, because we can't get enough of Him."*

Spiritual formation is all about becoming more like the Master, Jesus Christ. It's all about growing in intimacy with God and letting the Holy Spirit transform us into the image of Christ. If we read the Bible without encountering the Author, we have missed the whole point of reading the Bible in the first place. Without engaging the Author, reading the Bible indeed can be a dry, stale, lifeless process. But when we see the Bible as a means to a dynamic relationship with God, we can't get enough of the Bible, because we can't get enough of Him.

Making holy habits

If these three "R"s are the key to keeping the Bible at the center of our spiritual formation efforts, we must never permit them to languish. They must become holy habits. They sound simple, but so is breathing—simple and essential.

Reading the Bible once is not enough to make much progress toward spiritual maturity. Once we spend some time in God's Word today, we can look with anticipation to tomorrow when we can hit the "Refresh" button, bring it all back and start again.

While most Christ-followers have never read the Word all the way through once, it is the consistent, faithful, daily, meaningful, forever reading of the Word, with each of the attendant "R"s, that brings genuine spiritual formation.

I never tire of the advice from J. I. Packer. In his introduction to R. C. Sproul's book, *Knowing Scripture*. Packer observes: "If I were the devil, one of my first aims would be to stop folk from digging into the Bible. Knowing that it is the Word of God, teaching men to know and love and serve the God of the Word, I should do all I could to surround it with the spiritual equivalent of pits, thorn hedges, and man traps, to frighten people off. . . . At all costs I should want to keep them from using their minds in a disciplined way to get the measure of its message."[26]

Simply put: read the Bible, keep reading it, and read it again. One of the benefits of continually refreshing ourselves with God's Word is that we can continually make it personal this way. To clarify—the Bible is about God, not about us. But when we read the Bible, we'll find it much more meaningful if we find ourselves in the text. Make it personal. That means constantly asking questions such as: "How would I respond to that?" or "What if that were me?" or even "That describes me. What should I do?"

Seeing yourself in God's Word

German theologian Helmut Thielicke used to tell his students that they should read the Word to find themselves in it. To illustrate what he meant, Thielicke would tell them of his young son who, when just a tiny baby, he would hold in front of a mirror. When the baby would wave his arms, the reflection waved. When he kicked his feet, his reflection kicked. Suddenly the boy's face lit up when he realized *that's me!*

That's how the Bible lights up our faces too—when we realize that we aren't simply reading stories or parables or doctrine or history. We are reading about us. God interacts with us through the pages of Scripture. He continually invites us to get to know Him more, the God of the universe, so that we can reflect His glory and bring honor to Him.

It's a wonderful thought. Really, it's the message of the Bible. God so loved the world that He sent His Son to die for us. Whoever believes in Him won't perish, but have everlasting life. The Bible shows us this pathway. God comes to us, and invites us to participate in His spectacular plan.

It's almost too wonderful for words.

CHAPTER 9

The Searching Fields of Contemporary Spirituality

Throughout this book I have spoken of marginalizing the Bible. There is more to come. However, I want to switch gears in the next several chapters before we return to the Bible as God's chosen method of communicating with us. A lack of intimacy with God through His Word has led many to a perceived need for "something else." Bible illiteracy has produced a deepening search for spirituality in non-biblical, non-orthodox, and non-satisfying ways. Think through a list of people you know (professing Christians or otherwise), and consider what you've observed, or what they've expressed—good and bad—about their spirituality.

- Perhaps you have a friend who's stated main goal while exercising at a gym is "to find inner peace."
- Or you have a cousin who used to be a Baptist; he's now attending an Eastern Orthodox Church and says he finds a greater sense of fulfillment in icons and rituals.
- Or maybe your neighbor returned to the Roman Catholic Church as a result of the "Catholics Come Home" television campaign of 2010.
- Or the "I'm a Mormon" TV campaign of 2011 has your brother-in-law thinking, "They seem like nice people" and is considering becoming a Latter Day Saint.
- Or you have a carpool friend who's intrigued by the mystical teachings of Kabbalah.
- Or perhaps you lead a small group at church and find that the participants, all professing Christians, have a mixed bag of beliefs cherry-picked from a variety of religions.

Why the sudden interest in the 31 flavors of spirituality?

On a spiritual quest

It seems that everybody today is on some kind of spiritual quest. People are searching for something. There's a spiritual void, and most everyone can feel it. These longings are natural and actually originate from God. It's what people do with these longings that warrants our attention. There are many searching fields that promise spiritual fulfillment, but contrary to popular belief, these paths don't all lead to the same destination, and they are certainly not all sure paths. Some paths lead to confusion, some are very dangerous. Those of us who are teachers want to help people within our sphere of influence discern truth from error. But all of us want to make sure we're on the right path to fulfill our own spiritual longings.

Let's examine from a bird's eye perspective the burgeoning offerings of modern day spirituality to see what we're up against. The twelve most prevalent of today's spiritual searching fields are as follows.

1) Hindu spirituality

Swami Vivekananda is the main disciple of the 19th century mystic Ramakrishna and the founder of Ramakrishna Mission. He is chiefly responsible for introducing Vedanta and Yoga in Europe and America. According to Vivekananda, the important lesson he received from Ramakrishna was that "Jiva is Shiva"[27] ("each individual is divinity itself"). This became his Mantra and is the spiritual lesson of Yoga.

Some of the main beliefs of Hinduism are:

- All of life is unity—every form of life is connected to every other form of life.
- Every birth is a rebirth; the doctrine of reincarnation is non-negotiable.
- Karma is non-negotiable; do your best and don't worry about the consequences.
- The spiritual goal of everyone is that *Atman* (your essential self, the inner-most essence of the individual) needs to be liberated in human life.
- The more you meditate, the more you discover the divine—it is you.

As you may remember, ex-Beatle George Harrison died chanting the Hare Krishna Mahamantra in the company of Hindu monks.

2) Buddhist spirituality

Buddhism is the fourth-largest religion in the world behind Christianity, Islam, and Hinduism. The religion is actually a family of beliefs and practices based on the teachings of Siddhartha Gautama, commonly known as "The Buddha" (the Awakened One).

Unlike many religions, Buddhism has no single central text that is universally accepted by all Buddhism's faith traditions. Thus, while meditation is huge in Buddhism, it is not meditation through or even upon a sacred text. Buddhist meditation is fundamentally concerned with transforming the mind and using it to explore itself. Spiritual formation in the most common forms of Buddhism is discovered internally, by discovering yourself and your place in the world around you.[28]

3) **Zen spirituality**

Like other forms of Buddhism, Zen places little emphasis on sacred scriptures. But one key element of spiritual formation in Zen Buddhism is the teaching that we must empty ourselves of all thoughts in order to penetrate the realm of the True Self, which is equated with the Buddha himself. According to Zen master, Kosho Uchiyama, "When we let go of thoughts and wake up to the reality of life that is working beyond them, we discover the Self . . . that pervades all living creatures and all existence."[29]

In Zen teaching spiritual formation is achieved through meditation in which we free ourselves from external thoughts (such as sacred texts or written codes) in order to achieve direct realization by connecting with the ultimate reality (i.e. God).

> *"One key element of spiritual formation in Zen Buddhism is the teaching that we must empty ourselves of all thoughts in order to penetrate the realm of the True Self, which is equated with the Buddha himself."*

4) **Jewish spirituality**

The search for spirituality in the religious practices of Judaism, although not limited to it, is primarily evidenced in the teachings of Kabbalah (also spelled *Kabala* and *Cabbala*). Kabbalah means "received tradition" and is concerned with the mystical aspect of Judaism.

According to Kabbalistic tradition, the Kabbalah records the secrets that God revealed to Adam, secrets transmitted orally by the Patriarchs, sages and prophets. From about the 10th century BC onward foreign conquests drove the Jewish spiritual leadership (the Sanhedrin) underground and forced them to hide this knowledge. As a result, the Kabbalah became secretive, forbidden, and cryptic to Judaism for two and a half millennia.

In the twenty-first century, however, the ancient, secret mysteries of the Jews have gone high tech and Hollywood. There is a 24-hour, non-stop Kabbalah channel in Israel. Also available online, it features regular guests including prominent figures from Israel and Hollywood.

5) **Muslim spirituality**

Sufism is the inner, mystical dimension of Islam. A practitioner of this tradition is generally known as a ṣūfī, although many in the West know them by the word dervish. I have met many of the famous "whirling dervishes" in my travels in central Turkey.

Sufism, or "Islamic Mysticism," is the religious subset of Muslims who seek divine knowledge through a direct personal experience which leads to mystical union with ultimate reality. Sufis believe that only the direct knowledge of God can satisfy the struggle for spirituality. Sufis also believe that ultimate reality is attained through subjective experience, not through the writings of a sacred text.

6) **Native American spirituality**

Much of the spirituality of First Nation peoples, Native Americans, or Indians (the designation largely depends on the region and a non-Indian perspective) centers around the Shaman, the Aboriginal healer or spiritual leader. To the beating of drums and chanting, the Shaman invites the spirits to enter his body during public lodge ceremonies. Sometimes Shamans claim they enter into a trance and travel to the underworld or go to distant places seeking healing or spirituality. In this respect, Native American spirituality is remarkably similar to channeling and other practices of New Age spirituality.

Native American spirituality is very naturalistic. Practitioners believe spirit creatures control the weather, hence the rain dance and other rituals. Practitioners also believe that animals were originally humans, and they share the same ancestors. But the key feature of Native American spirituality is the relationship of man to "Mother Earth." Much of Native American spirituality forms the basis for a kind of "green spirituality" that became so popular in the 20th century and continues today.

7) **Monastic spirituality**

Monasticism, literally the act of "dwelling alone," refers to the practice of living in seclusion. For the monks or others living in a monastic community, the goal is to know God more fully and love Him more deeply. They believe the isolation of desert life will teach them not to be concerned about the things of this world. In the pursuit of spiritual formation monks spend hours in contemplative prayer, repetition of liturgies, silence and solitude. Their path to spirituality is as much about what they do as what they deny for themselves.

The earliest Christian monastic communities were founded in the deserts of Egypt, most notably by the hermit St. Anthony of Egypt. Those who followed have become collectively known as "the Desert Fathers," the oft-quoted hermits, ascetics, and monks who lived mainly in the same Egyptian Nitrate desert as Anthony.

8) **"Modern" Roman Catholic spirituality**

Many Catholics truly follow Christ and are redeemed in the biblical sense of the word, yet some branches of Catholicism tend to promote additional allegiances other than Christ. For instance, when describing spiritual formation, one prominent Catholic educational group states: "Our goal is to foster a deep and genuine love for Jesus Christ, Mary, the Church, the Pope and the salvation of souls."[30]

For Catholics, spiritual formation often springs from the wisdom already said to be within an individual. As such, the Catholic struggle for spirituality relies heavily on practices and processes, namely on the exercise of disciplines practiced over hundreds of years of Catholicism.

9) **Mystic spirituality**

Mysticism is the pursuit of becoming one with God through direct experience. Like monasticism, mysticism is found in nearly every religion. Despite the various religious approaches to it, mysticism seems to exhibit some common characteristics in all religions. Philosopher W. T. Stace identified seven common themes of mysticism when studying Roman Catholic, Protestant, ancient classical, Hindu, and American agnostic mystical experiences.

- The unifying vision, expressed abstractly by the formula "All is One."
- The more concrete apprehension of the One as being an inner subjectivity in all things, described variously as life, consciousness, or a living Presence.
- Sense of objectivity or reality.

- Feeling of blessedness, joy, happiness, and satisfaction.
- Feeling that what is apprehended is holy, sacred, or divine. This is the quality which gives rise to the interpretation of the experience as being an experience of "God."
  - A paradoxical feeling, alleged by mystics to be ineffable, incapable of being described in words.
  - Alleged by mystics to be ineffable, incapable of being described in words, etc.[31]

Mysticism has become the super highway for many seeking the sure path to God, even among many Evangelicals.

10) **New Age spirituality**

New Age spirituality has no holy text, central organization, membership, formal clergy, geographic center, dogma, creed, or much of anything else by which you can define it. The New Age is more of a free-flowing spiritual movement that is often better described than defined. It's a combination of spirituality and superstition with roots traceable to many sources: Astrology, Channeling, Hinduism, Gnostic traditions, Spiritualism, Taoism, Theosophy, Wicca and other Neo-pagan traditions.

Ralph White, co-founder and creative director of the New York Open Center, writes, "Many people see themselves as living in a meaningless world, and there is a profound cry for meaning. We've seen that tendency in churches, because the way religion is presented traditionally has spoken to our inner selves less and less. People want a living, feeling experience of spirituality. They yearn to get in touch with the soul."[32]

11) **Spirituality without religion**

In past decades, people tended to link their spirituality to an organized religion or formally defined belief system, but that is not true anymore. Today, even atheists can be spiritualists.

Robert Wuthnow, Chair of the Department of Sociology and Director of the Princeton University Center for the Study of Religion and the author of the book *After Heaven: Spirituality in America Since the 1950s,* clarifies that there has been a shift in America from a spirituality based on "dwelling" to one based on "seeking." Dwelling emphasizes the importance of sacred places, such as the church, synagogue or mosque, and was more prevalent during times of social stability, a type of spirituality that typified the post-war period of the 1950s. In contrast, "seeking" focuses on individuals looking for sacred moments, which are fleeting, and negotiating "among complex and confusing meanings of spirituality."[33]

A 2009 poll from LifeWay Research emphasizes this trend. It found that nearly three of every four Millennials (ages 18 to 29)—call themselves *spiritual* but not *religious*. And while 65 percent of those surveyed called themselves *Christian*s, they rarely pray, read the Bible or go to church.

12) Secular spirituality

Secular spirituality is the cultural phenomenon that refers to the adherence to a spiritual ideology without a religious framework. In secular spirituality the emphasis is on practice rather than belief and on the inner peace of the individual rather than on a relationship with the divine. Secular spirituality emphasizes fulfillment and altruism, yet places little emphasis on anything "divine." The poster child for this non-religious spirituality is none other than the 44th President of the United States. "Barack Obama has become a symbol of the rise of secular spirituality in this country, a liberated set of values that exists largely outside organized religion,"[34] Indian-born author and lecturer Deepak Chopra noted on his blog.

Chopra listed President Obama's principles of secular spirituality. They included:

- A spiritual duty to be benign stewards of the Earth and to preserve the ecology.
- A duty to further peace among nations.
- A sense of compassion for the poor and wretched beset by pandemic disease, lack of political influence, and denial of basic human rights.

Secular spirituality has become a national phenomenon that Chopra predicts "will swell steadily in the coming years, particularly among the young."

These are the main searching fields for spirituality presented to your neighbors, your co-workers and your family. Some may seem a little far-fetched to you, but thousands of Christians who are unsatisfied with the traditional biblical answers to life's struggles have migrated to elements of these religious and non-religious options.

You don't have to look hard to find someone you know who has sought spiritual sanctuary in one of these spiritual searching fields.

CHAPTER 10

Salad Bar Spirituality

Recently I watched an interview on *60 Minutes* where a well-known singer described herself as a "Buddhist-Baptist." The singer explained how she had been raised Baptist, but converted to Buddhism in later life, retaining many of her Christian beliefs and practices. In her mind, the two circles of thought were very close. She told how she held to the foundations of the Ten Commandments and to many principles Christ taught, yet she also felt that "just about every problem in life" could be solved by daily chanting and other Buddhist principles.

This singer is an example of an increasing and disturbing trend. People are hungry for truth, yet in their quest for truth they mix and match faith traditions, truth and non-truth. They might jump from one religion to the next (and often back again). Or they might not entirely convert from one religion to another, but will "borrow" whatever type of spirituality appeals to them and blend it all together.

I call this trend "salad bar spirituality." At a salad bar you can pick and choose any items you want. Three different kinds of lettuce. Six different kinds of cheese. Piles of bean sprouts or chopped eggs. You take a big plate and pile it high. When it comes to faith, so many religions, belief systems, and spiritual options are offered that a person doesn't know what's best, so he or she takes a little of this and a little of that. In essence, a person creates his or her own form of spirituality. They might mix orthodoxy with chanting, or a little Methodism with monasticism. Their faith becomes a pile of whatever looks most appetizing, just like their plate at the tail end of a salad bar.

> *"The trend of 'salad bar spirituality' is actually not new. Historically, this has been called religious syncretism."*

Researchers have shown this trend in action. The Pew Research Center's Forum on Religion & Public Life released an extensive study of this phenomenon[35] in 2009, and found:

- One third of Americans describe themselves as church hoppers, often attending religious services at more than one place, and often services of a faith different from their own.
- More than one in five Christians believes in reincarnation.
- Almost a quarter of all Christians believe in astrology, and roughly the same number believe that spiritual energy is located in physical things such as mountains, trees, and crystals.

Evangelical pastors and church leaders often do not know how to reverse this trend within their congregations. Sometimes they are oblivious to the trend. Sadly, at times they even embrace it. I contend that we need to be very aware that Evangelicals are borrowing freely from other faith traditions, and that the trend is ultimately very deadly. I propose something can be done. The solution begins with a solid awareness of the issues at stake, and—most importantly—a solid grasp of truth.

Searching for a spiritual buzz

The trend of salad bar spirituality is actually not new. Historically, this has been called *religious syncretism*. It describes the combination of different forms of belief or practice, or even the attempted reconciliation of differing systems of spirituality. It's been shown to occur in situations where foreign beliefs are introduced to an indigenous belief system and the teachings are blended.

Historical examples include:

- **Ancient Greece**. Gods were often adopted into the pantheon of Greek deities simply by changing their names from another culture's gods. For example, the Egyptian god Amun became the Greek god Zeus.
- **Rome.** Like the Greeks did with the Egyptians, the Romans adopted Greek deities. The Greek god Dionysus became the Roman god Bacchus, Poseidon became Neptune, as well as many others.
- **The Caribbean.** In the age of European imperialism, three outcomes of the fusion of European and African religions were the Rastafarian movement, (founded in Jamaica), Voodoo, (prevalent in Haiti), and Santería, (found throughout the Caribbean).

- **South America.** When the Roman Catholic Church attempted to evangelize South America, the animistic religion the natives had formerly practiced was never fully replaced. It was simply blended with Catholic teachings. Thus Catholicism in South America today is heavily laced with animism, spiritism and paganism.

Likewise, we see widespread examples of syncretism today, even to the point where meshed belief systems become classified as mainstream religions. Syncretism is popular as an ideology because it appears to facilitate coexistence and constructive interaction between different cultures. Conversely, those who reject spiritual syncretism today are often labeled biased, bigoted or hate-mongers. Examples of modern day syncretism include:

- **Unitarian Universalism**, which traces its roots to Universalist and Unitarian Christian congregations.
- **Chrislam**, or *The Will of God Mission* or *Ifeoluwa Mission*. This is a Nigerian syncretic religion that mixes elements of Christianity and Islam, as the name implies. Founded by Tela Tella in the 1980s, the sect predominantly exists in Lagos, Nigeria.
- **The Unification Church of Korea**. Its leader, the late Sun Myung Moon, openly confessed that his religion, although primarily Christian, integrated key components of Buddhism and Confucianism.

Evangelicals might read this list and believe the trend has not seeped into orthodox Christianity, but evidence shows that in our quest for meaningful spirituality, many Evangelicals have simply abandoned our rich heritage of *sola scriptura* and directly borrowed from other faith traditions. Many Evangelicals are looking elsewhere for a spiritual buzz. Christianity's increased willingness to draw from Eastern religions and mysticism has caused us to demonstrate a dangerous selective forgetfulness of God's Word.

But I'm a Christ-follower: where do I go?

In light of the many options at the spiritual salad bar, the question naturally arises: where does an Evangelical go for spiritual formation? That question specifically was the title of an open thread I was reading on an Internet forum some time back.

The specific question was posed this way, with a touch of humor:

"Imagine that a Baptist (or other Evangelical) were to decide that he wanted to deepen his spiritual life, grow spiritually, seek out spiritual direction, and pursue spiritual formation. Where would he go within his own Evangelical, Protestant tradition to find resources, guidance, or direction? (Okay—I can hear the Catholics and Orthodox giggling already. Cut it out.) Before I leave the open thread to you readers, let me say that this is a real problem."[36]

Two responses (from real people) particularly interested me:

- "Several of my friends and myself have exited mainstream Evangelicalism. I went Reformed. My friend, who is a pastor, has gone Emerging/house church, and another has replaced it with self-study and monasticism. Some of the people that I know have gone full-on Catholic."
- "I think a big problem in this area is that Evangelicals as a cultural group don't actually desire the presence of God, though of course many members and congregations do. But what we desire on the whole is to have successful institutions."

Even those who see themselves as Christ-followers and who believe the Bible is the actual Word of God are still struggling with making any headway on the road toward spiritual maturity. Brad Waggoner, president of B&H Publishing Group, and a team of researchers from the Southern Baptist Convention (the largest Evangelical denomination in America), conducted a series of surveys over 2007 and 2008 to determine how Protestant churchgoers are faring in their spiritual development. They discovered that in a year's time only about 3.5 percent of respondents showed a regular, demonstrable level of spiritual growth. [37] Why so little spiritual progression? See chapter 2.

A 2008 Barna survey perhaps pinpointed the problem.[38] Essentially, the survey found that Christians were clearly interested in relating to others at church and serving others outside of church, but their interest in becoming closer to God and growing in grace and knowledge of Jesus Christ was highly lacking. Why so little progress on the road toward spiritual maturity? See chapter 2.

To me, the results of those surveys are staggering. We're engaging in fellowship and service to a good extent, and that's fine, but we're missing out on study and application. We see evidences of this all the time within churches today. The Evangelical church has it all together on worship. We can sing, clap, and dance with the best of them. We have learned how to bond and build relationships through small groups. We have spent boatloads of cash to pay our way on short-term mission trips to serve others. We have let ourselves be inundated with a host of mystic voices—religious and non-religious alike—about how to grow spiritually. But we're still missing true spiritual maturity. Why? We are not engaging God's Word in a consistent, meaningful way.

Some of these practices are, of course, not wrong. But the point is that we still lack a coherent strategy to grow spiritually. These surveys indicate that the *bulk* of Evangelicals seem to have made little progress on the road toward true spiritual maturity and that fact needs to haunt us. Surely there are many inhibiters to personal spiritual formation, but as the research survey in Chapter Two clearly showed, none are more formidable than a lack of Bible engagement. Evangelicals aren't experiencing spiritual growth the way they want because they aren't receiving, reflecting on and responding to the Bible the way God wants!

John and Jane

I'll call them John and Jane Smith.

Several years ago they contacted the ministry I served as president, *Back to the Bible,* to tell us that two years before they had become Christians, which we were very happy to hear. They wanted to tell us the rest of their story.

As soon as they decided to follow Christ, they were excited at their new-found faith, and a natural question immediately arose: how could they grow in their faith? How could they—in the words of Paul—become fully "mature in Christ" (Colossians 1:28), no longer infants in their spiritual thinking and behavior, but with faith that is developed, healthy, and strong? Spiritual maturity is an admirable goal, one that Scripture urges people toward. It's where people are personally, vitally, and organically united with Christ in the same way branches are linked to a vine and draw their strength for growth from the vine. This couple's desire to become spiritually mature was sincere. They professed a genuine love for Christ and wanted to follow Him wholeheartedly. So what were they supposed to do next?

Fortunately, John and Jane came to Christ as part of the outreach ministry of a trusted Evangelical church that offered a variety of other ministries. John and Jane eagerly joined a small group and quickly immersed themselves in the overall life of their spiritual community. They began to have spiritual discussions and learn the value of prayer. They started understanding what worship is all about. They read books by Christian authors. They invested time in helping the poor; they tithed; they attended men's and women's retreats; they even learned to fast.

They were doing everything they needed to do, right? At least that's what we thought.

Well, not so quick, they said, and they continued their story.

Mixed in with the teaching and discipleship that John and Jane received at their church was a new breed of spiritual formation practices, the new Christian spirituality. But many of these practices aren't new at all. Recently these practices have become more accepted and even encouraged by mainstream Evangelical churches, so we hear more about them today and it only seems that they're new. These practices are often presented to believers as helpful and trusted pathways to grow deeper in their faith.

John attended a men's group where he was encouraged to learn contemplative prayer. Jane was invited to attend a weekly fitness class at her church where all the Christian women enjoyed Yoga. John and Jane's pastor blogged daily, and one of his posts discussed in detail the benefits of connecting deeply with God while walking a labyrinth. One Sunday the church's spiritual formation pastor spoke from the front of the church about an exciting and enriching new way to read the Bible called *lectio divina*.

John and Jane weren't quite sure what all these practices were about, but they were eager to grow, and there was already a natural trust built into the process. The couple assumed that since these activities sounded like the spiritual thing to do, and because they were being practiced at their church, and because their pastor loved the Lord, then they were doing all the right things to grow spiritually.

But were they? John and Jane had contacted us to lament that they didn't think they were on the right path. They wanted help. They truly yearned to grow spiritually, but they felt spiritually empty and suspected that little had changed in their lives over the past two years.

I invite you to consider their question carefully, for it's a question all Christians need to ask either for themselves or for those they lead in their sphere of influence— by subscribing to this new Christian spirituality, were John and Jane Smith on the sure path toward spiritual maturity? Don't be too quick to answer.

CHAPTER 11

Traditional Spiritual Disciplines

I was not much of an athlete in high school. Sure, I was on the track team for three years and one season even went out for football. Except for a 19' 6" long jump in one meet, my athletic career was mediocre at best. But I tried hard. I remember the summer I went out for football, the first week of practice was designed for simple conditioning. Basically, all we did was run, and run, and run. I felt like Forrest Gump, only slower.

After a while, however, the coaches broke us up into squads depending on the position we would play. The offense had one set of disciplines; the defense another. The running backs did certain drills; the offensive line did others. Each coach had solidified in his own mind what disciplines were best for us and we followed their lead.

This book is not about the spiritual disciplines, but about the quintessential spiritual discipline—engaging God through His Word. My goal is to raise your awareness of how we have been marginalizing the Bible in our search for spiritual significance and to rouse you to make real progress on your personal quest for spiritual maturity. I would be remiss, however, if I alluded to the spiritual disciplines without at least telling you what they are. So, here goes.

The problem is, not many agree on what the spiritual disciplines actually are. Authors are like football coaches. They all have developed their own list of disciplines and drills. I want you to know that there are many good spiritual disciplines other than Bible reading—and perhaps in this book so far it sounds as though I do not believe this. But true and helpful spiritual disciplines do exist, and if they are sanctioned by God, they are all rooted in the Bible.

True spiritual disciplines, writes seminary professor Donald S. Whitney, are "those personal and corporate disciplines that promote spiritual growth. They are the habits of devotion and experiential Christianity that have been practiced by the people of God since biblical times."[39]

Going back to the beginning

It's important to note in Whitney's definition that spiritual disciplines "have been practiced by the people of God since biblical times." In this definition, spiritual disciplines are the normal practices of the sincere Christ-follower's life and are exhibited by people as far back as biblical times. I have read many authors from the emergent church talking about "ancient-future" or "vintage Christianity," that by going back in church history we will discover experiences that will help us go forward in the 21st Century Church. But for many of these writers going back means going back to the Desert Fathers of the 4th Century. Problem is, they don't go back far enough; they should go back all the way to the 1st century and adopt spiritual disciplines as they are taught in God's Word, not the Desert Fathers. Genuine spiritual disciples are not magical, mystical, or mythical practices; they are the everyday, Bible-based habits of those who are already moving down the road toward spiritual maturity.

Spiritual seekers are admonished to be and do and try so many things these days, how do you know which disciplines are beneficial to you and which are a crock? Equally important, when you read your favorite spiritual formation authors, everyone seems to have a different list of spiritual disciplines. How can that be? The simple answer is that there are many lifestyle habits in the Bible that are associated with becoming conformed to the image of Christ. So people tend to pick and choose.

For instance, in Richard Foster's classic book on spiritual formation, *Celebration of Discipline*, he lists twelve disciplines:

Part I. The Inward Disciplines
1. Meditation
2. Prayer
3. Fasting
4. Study

Part II. The Outward Disciplines
5. Simplicity
6. Solitude
7. Submission
8. Service

Part III. The Corporate Disciplines
9. Confession

10. Worship
11. Guidance
12. Celebration[40]

Arguably, Foster's writings have had the greatest impact related to the current emphasis on spiritual formation in the church today. Many pastors and their people now religiously follow the above outline of incorporating these spiritual disciplines into their lives. Although I don't agree with everything Foster says, I don't think there is a single discipline in his list that any Christian could argue is unbiblical. Given the right emphasis, each one would find support in God's Word.

> ***"Spiritual disciplines that are biblical are not magical, mystical, or mythical practices; they are the everyday, Bible-based habits of those who are already moving down the road toward spiritual maturity."***

The late Dallas Willard, perhaps the most prolific writer on spiritual formation, lists the core disciplines a bit differently. While many of the same disciplines appear in Willard's list, some newones appear as well.

Disciplines of Abstinence
Solitude
Silence
Fasting
Frugality
Chastity
Secrecy
Sacrifice

Disciplines of Engagement
Study
Worship
Celebration
Service
Prayer

Fellowship
Confession
Submission[41]

Other authors identify, group, and list the spiritual disciplines differently. My point is that many disciplines are beneficial. But there is one discipline—Bible engagement—that should be at the top of every list, and often isn't.

Some curious omissions

Incidentally, I find it odd that the lists that New Testament writers often referred to are conspicuously absent in many of today's popular author's treatment of spiritual disciplines. For example, on what lists do Peter's admonitions in 1 Peter 3:8 to "have unity of mind, sympathy, brotherly love, a tender heart, and a humble mind" appear?

What about the Apostle Paul's list in Romans 12:9-21? Note the injunctions as taken directly from the biblical text:

- Hate what is evil; cling to what is good.
- Be devoted to one another in love.
- Honor one another above yourselves.
- Never be lacking in zeal, but keep your spiritual fervor, serving the Lord.
- Be joyful in hope.
- [Be] patient in affliction.
- [Be] faithful in prayer.
- Share with the Lord's people who are in need.
- Practice hospitality.
- Bless those who persecute you; bless and do not curse.
- Rejoice with those who rejoice; mourn with those who mourn.
- Live in harmony with one another.
- Do not be proud, but be willing to associate with people of low position.
- Do not be conceited.
- Do not repay anyone evil for evil.
- Be careful to do what is right in the eyes of everyone. If it is possible, as far as it depends on you, live at peace with everyone.
- Do not take revenge, my dear friends, but leave room for God's wrath, for it is written: 'It is mine to avenge; I will repay,' says the Lord. On the contrary: If your enemy is hungry, feed him; if he is thirsty, give him something to drink. In doing this, you will heap burning coals on his head.
- Do not be overcome by evil, but overcome evil with good

Some of the issues Paul raises about living a life as disciplined by the Holy Spirit undoubtedly would be incorporated into today's popular lists of spiritual disciplines, but others are left out completely. We have to wonder why. Why is solitude a spiritual discipline but "honor one another above yourselves" not?

Perhaps most glaring of all the omissions by many authors is the greatest list of spiritual disciplines that we know as the fruit of the Spirit listed in Galatians 5:22-24. Why don't we see a book penned by a popular spirituality leader today that encourages Christians to learn the practical and biblical disciplines of:

- love
- joy
- peace
- patience
- kindness
- goodness
- faithfulness
- gentleness
- self-control

I realize that books are outlined and written for a lot of different reasons. But while it is commendable that almost every writer on spiritual disciplines mentions the need for engaging the Bible as one of the disciplines, and some even say it is the most important discipline, almost all authors immediately dismiss the Bible as so evident to the process of spiritual formation that they barely need to talk about it.

But we *do* need to talk about it.

Many people, even those practicing spiritual disciplines, do not read their Bible and thus remain blissfully unaware of all the Bible's guidance for living the Christ-like life we are striving for.

CHAPTER 12

Prayer Practices With Some Baggage

The spiritual disciplines mentioned in the last chapter can help us progress down the road to spiritual maturity. They must not be permitted, however, to minimize the importance of the three "R"s of reading, reflecting and responding to God's Word. But there are some so-called spiritual disciplines that I think should come with warning labels on them.

For the past decade or so, I've become increasingly concerned. I want Christians everywhere to understand that it is possible to progress on a sure path toward maturity in their faith, and engaging the Bible meaningfully and consistently is that sure path. My urgent desire is that people with similar stories as John and Jane Smith grow to be like Christ. What I don't want is for believers to settle for some mystical, monastic, misleading concept of spirituality. People need to be able to judge what's handed to them. They need to be able to discern what they're reading from Christian authors and hearing from Christian leaders. And they need the tools to discern whether or not some popular spiritual practices are truly biblical spiritual practices.

To that end, in this chapter and the next, let's take a bird's eye view of some of the contemporary spiritual practices that not only are attractive to Evangelicals, but also are being pirated by them and amalgamated into both our church services and our spiritual lives. But these practices should come with a flashing caution light. Two of them are prayer practices. They deserve your serious investigation. And with that serious investigation you may wonder why your church has already adopted them. Here are two prayer practices that, at the very least, have a past to deal with and bring some baggage with them to the spiritual formation table.

Practice #1: Contemplative Prayer

A few years back, a friend of mine frequently gathered with a group of Christian pastors and parachurch leaders to pray together. When it was his turn to pray, this man would first take a very long time to say anything. It was beyond simply focusing his mind or gathering his thoughts. Several full minutes of dead air would pass. Then, the man would begin praying by saying:

Jesus, Jesus, Jesus, Jesus, Jesus, Jesus, Jesus, Jesus . . .

Or sometimes,

Holy, holy, holy, holy, holy, holy, holy, holy, holy, holy, holy . . .

The man didn't have a stutter.

He'd been to a conference in California that taught him how to pray this way, he explained, and that silence and repetition of a sacred word helped him focus his mind and thoughts. He wasn't speaking in tongues or a "prayer language." He was an Evangelical who had been told that certain types of prayer could develop a person's relationship with Jesus Christ in ways where a person communed with God *beyond* words, thoughts, feelings, and actions.

Part of his ministry at the church involved youth work, and he was training high school kids to use these same prayer techniques. He encouraged the pastors to learn the technique as well, so they could teach their congregations. What would you say to this man? Would you join in prayer with him, perhaps learn his techniques, and use the same methods he did? Would you want him leading the youth in your church, and invite him to teach a guest study for your small group or congregation?

Or, would you be wary? You might still pray with him, but would you adopt his techniques as your own?

What is contemplative prayer?

What the man displayed were two types of praying that have become popular in the new Christian spirituality movement: contemplative prayer and centering prayer. The language of these movements often looks good up front. Instructors claim that the practices provide Christians with a deeper sense of the will of God, or of the love of God. Those benefits provide strong draws to people's natural sense of wanting more intimacy with God, and Evangelicals are becoming practitioners of these types of praying in record numbers. But do they really know what they are doing? We must dig into these practices to discern what's under the surface.

One Christian website introduces practitioners to the subject this way:

> "During contemplative prayer we center our full attention on the presence of God, on the will of God, and on the love of God. Contemplative prayer is centered on faith in the Lord Jesus Christ, by which we can know the presence of God in very real ways.
>
> We come before God and see Jesus with the eyes of our heart as we adore and worship God in quiet, silent prayer.
>
> When we practice contemplative prayer we stay quiet before the Lord and wait longingly for God. 'Be still and know that I am God' (Psalm 46:10)." [42]

See what I mean about the attractive language? What Christian wouldn't want what this website is offering?

Contemplative prayer usually involves sitting comfortably, with eyes closed, and maintaining perfect silence, except for sometimes saying a sacred word repeatedly in order to focus on God during the exercise. Simply put, contemplative prayer is prayer without words. It is silent prayer in which one removes conscious thought from the mind, stills the ego, and attempts simply to exist in the presence of the Holy Spirit, asking of God nothing but His presence.

But as much as some in the contemplative prayer movement want us to see God as "silent and empty," throughout this book we have seen that the Bible presents quite a different view of God. He is certainly not silent and He is complete, full of all that it takes to be the Sovereign God of the Universe.

No empty words in biblical prayers

Overall, prayers, as modeled in the Bible, are significantly different from the contemplative approach being championed today. For instance, Matthew 5 instructs us to pray for our enemies and to pray without making a show. Mathew 7 tells us to not to use "empty phrases" or be repetitious with "many words" when we pray, and to pray that God would send workers into His harvest. Matthew 21:22 and James 1:6 tell us to pray in faith. Luke 18:1-8 encourages us to pray without giving up. In John 16:23-24 we are told to pray in Jesus' name, and in Romans 8:25-27 we are given confidence that the Holy Spirit prays for us when we don't know how to pray. 1 Corinthians 14:15 tells us to pray with both the spirit and the mind, and 1 Thessalonians 5:17 encourages us to pray without stopping even when we don't get answers.

Ironically, there is an example in the Bible of a prayer with empty words, repetitious words, words that produce more heat than light and, come to think of it, not much heat. At the contest between the Prophet Elijah and the prophets of Baal on Mount Carmel, Baal's bunch "called upon the name of Baal from morning until noon, saying, 'O Baal, answer us'" (1 Kings 18:26). They repeated that phrase over and over for hours, but to no avail. The only biblical example of a pattern of prayer that resembles contemplative prayer is this pagan prayer of the prophets of Baal.

The Bible is clear that prayer makes use of words and thought. Prayer is not simply mindless meditation. The Word of God has been given to us for the very purpose of basing our faith, and our lives, on its truth, the truth of God (2 Timothy 3:16-17). Trusting in mystical or experiential knowledge over the biblical record takes us outside the boundaries of truth established by God in His Word.

Three questions of contemplative prayer

There are three questions Evangelicals must raise with regard to contemplative prayer:

Question 1: Is *silence* actually the language of God?

One of the core themes of the contemplative prayer movement is that "Silence is the language of God." This quote is attributed to Father Thomas Keating, the Trappist monk who was one of the architects of centering prayer as a form of contemplative prayer, but does it correspond with Scripture, or with some other spiritual tradition?

Take a look at similar quotes.

- "Silence is the language of God; it is also the language of the heart." – *Swami Sivananda Saraswati* (1887-1963), a Hindu spiritual teacher and proponent of Sivananda Yoga and Vedanta.
- "Silence is the great teacher, and to learn its lessons you must pay attention to it. There is no substitute for the creative inspiration, knowledge, and stability that come from knowing how to contact your core of inner silence" — *Deepak Chopra*, author, doctor, and speaker who perpetuates Transcendental Meditation, among other Eastern spiritual practices.
- "What exists in truth is the Self alone. The Self is that where there is absolutely no "I" thought. That is called Silence. The Self itself is the world; the Self itself is "I"; the Self itself is God" — *Ramana Maharshi*, Hindu teacher.

Certainly, one might argue that the same bit of truth can be mixed into more than one religion, so just because other religions state that silence is God's language, it still might be the truth. I'll acquiesce to that line of reasoning, but I mention the above quotes simply to show the uncanny similarities between Father Keating's philosophy of silence and Eastern thought.

It's also true that silence is not the enemy of Christianity. Silence, by and large, can be a good thing, soothing and comforting, and we can get deep insights when we are quiet.

My point, however, is that we simply cannot attribute the idea of silence being the language of God to the Bible. "Quiet" is not a one-for-one synonym with "prayer", and there is no biblical basis to show that real prayer is wordless. The teaching is simply not found in the Bible, regardless of how Psalm 46:10 is wrenched from its context. And the concept that God's language is silence is contradicted again and again in Scripture.

> *"Listen for God to speak where God has already spoken, not in silence, but in His revelation."*

Rather, the God of the Bible is shown to be a God who speaks. In my electronic concordance, a simple search of the phrase ". . .and God said . . ." shows that it's repeated 505 times in the Bible. God is a speaker, a God who reveals Himself. He spoke and inspired various authors to write down what He revealed about Himself.

So this first question must be rejected. Is "silence" the language of God? The answer is a resounding "no." If you want to get to know God and become more intimate with Him, then listen to Him, yes. But don't expect silence to be His voice. He has never proven Himself to work that way. Listen to what He tells you in His Word. Listen for God to speak where God has already spoken, not in silence, but in His revelation.

Questions 2: Is mindlessness the key to true meditation?

Practitioners of contemplative prayer are encouraged to void their minds of everything, but is this biblical teaching?

The late Thomas Merton, a Roman Catholic monk and mystic who was a poet, social activist and student of comparative religion, advocated a mind-emptying meditation that empties ourselves and loses ourselves in a void he interchangeably called "the life of the spirit," or "Nirvana."[43]

I would feel much more comfortable with this practice if the emphasis was on filling the mind rather than emptying it. Meditation that is biblical is always synonymous with thinking deeply about something. Christian meditation involves seeking deeper insights into God's Word (Psalm 1:2), pondering God Himself (Psalm 63:6), reflecting upon God's works (Psalm 77:12), and considering both what our responsibility is and what our response should be to His grace (1 Timothy 4:15).

Clearly, the Bible shows that knowledge of God comes from engaging God in Scripture, not from an empty head.

Question 3: Where does the idea of contemplative prayer originate?

There are no examples of people in the Bible emptying themselves so that they can draw near to God. So the question fleshes out like this: are there elements of contemplative prayer that cannot be explained other than by the influence of Eastern religions?

Consider the following:

- The process of emptying the mind is integral to Buddhist belief. The techniques of Transcendental Meditation involve emptying one's mind of distracting influences by reciting a Sanskrit word known as a "mantra," and engaging in an initiation rite that is in essence a Hindu worship ceremony.
- The use of a prayer word (or "sacred" word) to empty the mind, reach a mental void, and achieve pure consciousness in order to find God at the center, originates in Buddhism as well. Father Keating suggests that appropriate prayer words may be "Jesus", "Christos," "Jesus Christ," "Father," "Abba," "God," "Mother," "Mother Mary," "God Mother," "Amen," etc. But he also suggests that it is possible to use sacred words from other religious traditions such as "Shalom," "Salam," and "Allah."
- The state of pure consciousness is said to be the practice of emptying one's mind in order to experience an altered state of consciousness and, ultimately, direct contact with God. This is exactly what Hindus and Buddhists practice to reach what they call "god-consciousness."

I am not saying that all contemplative prayer is only a "Christianized" form of Eastern mysticism. It is evident, however, that the similarities between contemplative prayer and Eastern practice are much stronger than its similarities with biblical practice. In other words, if you want to dig in the soil that produced the concept of contemplative prayer, you must dig in the soil of India, not the soil of Israel.

Practice #2: Centering Prayer

Contemplative prayer and centering prayer are sometimes identified as the same practice, but on his organization's official website known as *Contemplative Outreach*, Thomas Keating, the father of centering prayer, distinguishes between the two: "Contemplative Prayer . . . is the opening of mind and heart—our whole being— to God, the Ultimate Mystery, beyond thoughts, words, and emotions. Centering prayer. . . is a movement beyond conversation with Christ to communion with Him."[44]

Again, on one hand, what Keating advocates sounds okay, even admirable. We want to open our whole being to God. We want to commune with Christ. Practitioners claim it originates from Jesus' Sermon on the Mount, but I can't find anything from Matthew 5-7 in this practice. Before we embrace any practice, we must look for warning signs that may indicate what seems highly spiritual may not always reflect biblical spirituality.

The revival of centering prayer can be credited to three Trappist monks: Thomas Keating, William Menninger, and Basil Pennington. In this method of praying, a person chooses a sacred word, which is repeated as often as needed to ignore all thoughts and feelings. The goal is to completely empty a mind so a person may experience the presence of God. Father Keating writes: "All thoughts pass if you wait long enough."[45]

When a mind is completely devoid of all thoughts, according to Keating, a person reaches a state of pure consciousness or a mental void. A person is then put into direct contact with God. Sometimes, in the midst of the consciousness, (often called "deeper levels of reality") a person will pick up "vibrations" that Father Keating says "were there all the time but not perceived." [46] The idea is that in centering prayer a person goes to the center of his being and there finds his true self. This process is supposed to dismantle the false self, which is supposedly the result of the emotional baggage a person carries.

The "mixed multitude" at the monastery

When Moses and the Israelites left behind their lives of slavery in Egypt, they did not leave the country alone. Exodus 12:38 records that "a mixed multitude went up with them," likely meaning Egyptians and other foreigners who were "hangers on" to the God of Israel. While treated kindly by Israel, these "outsiders" would eventually prove to be a detriment to God's people. Numbers 11:4 says they were the first to intensely lust what was left behind in Egypt and incited the Jews to grumble to God about the same.

Apparently Father Keating knew criticism would be coming with regard to the Eastern influence on his prayer practices, for in describing how the monks revived the practice, he admits to inviting a "mixed multitude" to inform him on the proper way to pray. He wrote:

> "We entertained a Zen master who wished to visit our monastery. We invited him to speak to the community and later to give a sesshin (a week-long intensive retreat). For nine years after that, he held sesshins once or twice a year at a nearby retreat house. We also were exposed to the Hindu tradition through Transcendental Meditation. Paul Marechal, a former monk of Holy Cross Abbey . . . had become a TM teacher and offered to instruct us in the practice. Exposure to these traditions, as well as conversations with visitors to our monastery who had benefited from them, naturally raised many questions in my mind as I tried to harmonize the wisdom of the East with the contemplative tradition of Christianity that I had been studying and trying to practice for thirty years." [47]

Catholic concerns

One might expect Evangelicals to express reservations about this mystical form of prayer but Catholics themselves have expressed concerns with the three monks' teaching. For instance, fellow Catholic Margaret A. Feaster writes, "In my [10-year] research on the New Age, I found that [centering prayer] is not Christian contemplation, and that this type of prayer is not recommended by Pope John Paul II, Cardinal Ratzinger, the Catechism of the Catholic Church, or St. Teresa of Avila."[48] In a full critique of the movement, Feaster concluded that the prayer word Father Keating recommends repeating during centering prayer to empty the mind of all thoughts and feelings is little different from the mantra of Eastern mystic religions.

Similarly, Catholic writer and journalist Johnnette Benkovic classifies centering prayer as the same as Transcendental Meditation. [49] Benkovic has interviewed people on her TV show and in her book who have done both centering prayer (CP) and Transcendental Meditation (TM). They claim it is basically the same. The only difference would be that in TM the mantras are names of Hindu gods, and in CP the sacred word is usually Jesus, God, peace, or love.

Father Finbarr Flanagan, who was involved in both centering prayer and transcendental meditation, said CP is basically TM in a Christian dress.[50]

The papacy has consistently expressed concerns about the centering prayer movement. Cardinal Joseph Ratzinger, (who is the former Pope Benedict XVI), has long been one of Roman Catholicism's most astute theologians. In his booklet, *Letter to the Bishops of the Catholic Church on Some Aspects of Christian Meditation*, he quotes his papal predecessor and says, "[John Paul II] said that the call of St. Teresa of Jesus advocating a prayer completely centered on Christ is valid even in our day, *against some methods of prayer which are not inspired by the gospel and which in practice tend to set Christ aside in preference for a mental void which makes no sense in Christianity.*"[51] [*italics* mine].

Additionally, the Pope's *Letter to the Bishops of the Catholic Church on Some Aspects of Christian Meditation* contains a section (III) entitled "Erroneous Ways of Praying" that reads like an expose of centering prayer.[52]

Evangelical concerns

If Roman Catholics have expressed concerns about the apparent similarities between Father Keating's practice of centering prayer and Eastern mystical and meditative practices, imagine the concerns that Evangelicals should have. Oddly, there are few such concerns, for many Evangelicals are embracing centering prayer in their search for spiritual significance rather than questioning it as their Catholic colleagues have.

So what legitimate concerns are expressed by those who hold the principles of *sola scriptura*? What do Bible-literate people see as the red flags to this approach to prayer?

To begin with, every concern already expressed in the Catholic community about centering prayer is equally a concern in the Protestant community. Yet Evangelicals have additional concerns, or at least they should. One of the most notable features of centering prayer is not what it adds but what it lacks, namely any biblical basis.

On his www.contemplativeoutreach.org website Father Keating suggests that people practice centering prayer twice daily for 20-30 minutes at a time. He also suggests it will deepen their relationship with God if they listen to the Word of God in Scripture and study *Open Mind, Open Heart*.[53]

Open Mind, Open Heart is Thomas Keating's 1986 "how to" book on centering prayer. It explains the origins of the prayer and discusses the difficulties a person may encounter with achieving interior silence. It never hurts to plug your own book when telling people how to deepen their relationship with God, but to include "listen" to Scripture and "study" *Open Mind, Open Heart* in the same line speaks volumes about the marginalization of the Bible in the centering prayer movement.

From bad to worse

Father Keating's disregard for the sacred text is even more egregious in his additions to Scripture. Leaving God's Word out of his theology and practice is bad enough, but to misquote it is far worse. Here are a couple of examples.

Keating quotes Jesus in Mark 8:34 as saying, "Unless you deny your *inmost* self and take up the cross, you cannot be my disciple." The monk added the word "inmost," which is not in the original text. In *Open Mind, Open Heart* he further comments, "Denial of our inmost self includes detachment from the habitual functioning of our intellect and will, which are our inmost faculties."[54]

This, of course, has nothing to do with what Jesus said or meant in Mark 8:34. Jesus was not teaching about mind-emptying; He was talking about obedience. Father Keating's need to find scriptural justification for his Eastern-laced prayer practice appears to have overridden his concern for the biblical injunction against adding to or taking away from Scripture (Revelation 22:18-19).

Another example of his light regard for the inspired text of Scripture is Keating's addition of two phrases to Luke 10:20 in his work, *Invitation to Love.* Father Keating paraphrases Jesus as saying, "Do not get excited about that kind of success. Anybody can work miracles with a little psychic energy and the divine assistance. What you should rejoice over is that your names are written in heaven."[55]

He uses this paraphrase to further undergird his teaching. But this passage is in the context of Jesus sending out His seventy-two disciples with the power to tread on serpents and scorpions in defeating the enemy. The Douay Version (Catholic Bible) at Luke 10:20 reads as follows. Jesus warns, "But yet rejoice not in this, that spirits are subject unto you; but rejoice in this, that your names are written in heaven."

Keating adds to the biblical text the references to working miracles "with a little psychic energy". These words do not occur in the original Greek nor would they ever appear in *any* version of the Bible (including the Douay). Jesus would never have suggested the use of "a little psychic energy," but that doesn't seem to bother Father Keating at all.

This disregard for the Bible, and in some cases, misuse of the Bible, should be enough to prompt Bible-believing Christians to think twice before adopting the Trappist's method of emptying the mind in order to fill the soul. There never was a full soul that did not have a full mind, filled with the mind of Christ.

CHAPTER 13

Labyrinths and Lectio Divina

People often argue that the validity of any spiritual discipline is what it means to them. How they use it. What adaptations in meaning or practice they have made to it. They're not concerned with where it came from or where it's going, they're only concerned with its existential meaning to them.

Sometimes adapting a practice is done with great success. At that Passover Seder supper the night He was betrayed, Jesus and His disciples gathered in an upper room to celebrate the beginning of the Passover. There Jesus gave new meaning to that old meal. He made the elements of the meal the elements of His ministry (Matthew 26:26-29). But was Jesus just adapting a Jewish feast for His own purposes? Not at all. Jesus came to fulfill the Law and He wasn't so much converting the Seder into the Lord's Supper as He was demonstrating the real meaning of the Seder (Matthew 5:17). We can't do that with the two "spiritual disciplines" examined in the last chapter or the two additional ones in this chapter.

Also growing in popularity are two "spiritual disciplines" that many people say they are simply adapting for their own benefit and not endorsing their past intended meaning. But most Christians who engage in these practices don't even know their origin or their intended meaning. Don't you think we should at least know a little of the history of a practice before we make it our own? Perhaps we'll choose not to make it our own.

We've already examined the first two such practices, let's examine three and four.

Practice #3: The a"mazing" labyrinth

You see them popping up everywhere—the prayer labyrinth. Basically, in the Christian context, a labyrinth is a maze-like path a person walks while praying and meditating. The exercise is designed to help people quiet their minds and draw them to God.

One explanation of the meaning of the labyrinth comes from the Lutheran Church Missouri Synod: "The labyrinth is a universal symbol for the world, with its complications and difficulties, which we experience on our journey through life. The entry to the labyrinth is birth; the center is death and eternal life. In Christian terms, the thread that leads us through life is divine grace. Like any pilgrimage, the labyrinth represents the inner pilgrimage we are called to make to take us to the center of our being."[56]

I said that a labyrinth is a "maze-like" path, but I need to clarify, because a labyrinth and a maze are not the same. A maze is a puzzle in the form of complex branching passages with choices of path and direction. Generally, a person walks through a maze and out the other side. With a labyrinth, a person has but one path that leads to the center. The purpose of the labyrinth is not to trick or confuse a person. It has a rather unambiguous through-route to the center and back and functions differently than a maze.

The popularity of labyrinths

To date, millions of people have walked labyrinths praying, contemplating, and meditating in order to deepen their commitment to God and broaden the scope of their understanding of Him. Many other labyrinths have less spiritual significance and can be found in schools, parks, medical centers, prisons, spas and even in people's backyards. Most that enjoy them do so in hopes of integrating the body with the mind and the mind with the spirit.

> *"Essentially, the labyrinth was little more than a device for earning salvation by works."*

The popularity of labyrinths has grown to the point where today you can download a labyrinth and walk the labyrinth on your computer screen with your cursor. There also is an online World Wide Labyrinth Locator to help people find the closest labyrinth in their area. And there are several Labyrinth Societies.

Writing for the National Catholic Reporter, Tim Unsworth notes the increased popularity of labyrinths. "Labyrinths are everywhere these days: They are on corporate logos, school T-shirts, and next to putting greens at the local country club. One can spot them on strategically placed tattoos. Churches galore are installing them on the back lawns of old rectories. One can find them on the mast-heads of parish bulletins or the backs of priests' chasubles. . . . Starbucks must have a labyrinthine-latte coffee that can have one walking in circles."[57]

Nothing new under the sun

Despite their recent popularity, labyrinths are nothing new. In Greek mythology, the labyrinth was an elaborate structure designed and built for King Minos of Crete. It was built so cunningly, that the builder could barely escape from it after he built it.

Around A.D. 77-79, Roman historian Pliny the Elder described the existence of four main labyrinths worldwide: the Cretan labyrinth, an Egyptian labyrinth, a Lemnian labyrinth, and an Italian labyrinth.

In the twelfth and thirteenth centuries, as with other pagan practices, the labyrinth became a central feature in many of the European Roman Catholic cathedrals and churches in the middle ages. The most famous of these remaining labyrinths is at Chartres Cathedral near Paris. Built around 1200, the cathedral adapted the use of the labyrinth so that it was walked as a symbolic pilgrimage or as an act of repentance. Essentially, the labyrinth was little more than a device for earning salvation by works, and by the 17th and 18th centuries, prayer labyrinths had lost much of their spiritual meaning.[58]

Describing the experience

When I have asked people why they walk the labyrinth, many cannot give an answer. Recently I asked two teen girls who walked the labyrinth at the United Methodist Church they attend why they did it and they just shrugged. They didn't have a clue. I've asked many adults about their experience in walking a labyrinth and, like beauty in the eye of the beholder, the answer seems to lie with the walker. What do people experience when they walk the labyrinth? The answer is pretty much whatever they want to experience. Some say they use this experience as a tool to draw closer to God. Some see it as an enhancement to contemplation. Others see it as good discipline, good exercise, or just plain fun.

Pastor Dan Kimball attended a National Pastor's Conference in San Diego where walking the labyrinth was offered as part of the worship experience. He wrote about the experience for *Leadership Journal:*

"The path was formed by black lines on a 35-foot square piece of canvas laid on the floor. We each were given a CD player with headphones to guide our journey through the 11 stations on the path. As we began the inward journey—toward the center of the canvas—a gentle female voice with a British accent read a portion of John 1. She told us not to rush through the labyrinth, but to slow down, breathe deeply, and fully focus on God. At the first stop, we looked at a television screen covered with complex, moving electronic wave forms. We were instructed to pray about and eliminate the noise within that interferes with God's voice. We dropped small stones into water, each stone representing a worry we were giving over to God. Later we drew on paper symbols of our hurts, prayed about each of them, and put them in a trash can.

After thirty minutes we found ourselves at the labyrinth's center, where, seated on cushions, we were offered the elements of Communion. The narrator read more Scripture and reminded us how near Jesus Christ is to us. There was a Bible if we desired to linger, reading and praying. The journey outward focused on how we can be used by God in other people's lives. At one station we made impressions of our hands and feet in a box of sand reminding us that we leave impressions on the people we touch.

My wife and I spent an hour in the labyrinth and found ourselves calmed and refreshed, our perspective uniquely restored. We made our own prayer path after the convention—we knew we couldn't keep this experience to ourselves."[59]

The Bible as an option

Don't miss this. Kimball says, "There was a Bible if we desired to linger . . . ." The labyrinth was designed to bring one closer to God, but God's ordained tool to reveal Himself and foster intimacy with Himself was there as an appendage. It was just optional. It was for anyone who wanted to linger. Talk about marginalizing the Bible!

Dan Kimball has drawn his share of criticism (particularly from bloggers on-line) for this practice, and I have to say that his experience is reflective of why books such as this one are important. They offer a counter-perspective. Pastor Kimball was seminary trained and appears to have a solid grasp of biblical fundamentals. Perhaps he was able to emerge from the experience of walking a labyrinth "calmed and refreshed" because he already has the Bible deeply rooted within him. But what about the other Christians who aren't as deeply grounded in Scripture?

My concern with prominent pastors engaging in such exercises is that, as Kimball did, they tend to recreate the experience for congregants at their churches back home. Kimball wrote, "Over two nights we saw more than 100 people go through the labyrinth. It was a joy to see so many people on their knees communing with God through the experiential prayer elements."[60]

Perhaps a case could be made that Kimball, whose church is located in Santa Cruz, California, is uniquely ministering to a subculture of Christians who respond to more nontraditional forms of artistic spiritual expression. But, from one pastor to another, I would rather have seen Kimball encourage his congregation to commune with God through the pages of Scripture, God's chosen vehicle, a proven means, rather than through an "experiential prayer element" such as a labyrinth, a very questionable means.

A veiled warning

The Lutheran Church Missouri Synod website, quoted earlier, concludes its piece on walking the labyrinth with these words:

> "Christians should be urged to exercise careful discernment in this area. They ought to be especially concerned about any practice that becomes a substitute for reflection on God's Word, prayer to Him for comfort and direction, and for guidance in the midst of life's problems and challenges. We are given the promise that spiritual enlightenment comes solely from the Holy Spirit who is active whenever we make use of the Word and the sacraments. The Holy Spirit draws us to Christ who is our Hope and Peace, and who gives us identity, purpose, and meaning in life. Christians, of course, need not reject external aids (e.g., art, crosses, prayer guides, etc.) as in themselves objectionable, but they will want to avoid allowing such external reminders to become a spiritual crutch or substitute for the real thing."[61]

Deeper concerns

Should the Evangelical church be concerned about things like walking the labyrinth becoming a spiritual crutch? Do people substitute these kinds of spiritual journeys to the center for the real thing—focusing on God by engaging Him in His Word? Absolutely. In fact, while any biblical practice used under the guidelines of Scripture can be a tool to grow spiritually, there is precious little reference to biblical guidelines in any of the items we have addressed thus far in this chapter. Instead, just the opposite is true.

When the practice of walking the labyrinth is observed outside Evangelical realms, the practice appears more clearly false. For instance, Reverend Jill

Geoffrion, a certified labyrinth facilitator and author of *Labyrinths and Praying the Labyrinth,* when dedicating a new labyrinth, suggested that those attending form a circle and extend "the energy that is in our hearts and minds through their hands towards the labyrinth."[62]

I find no biblical support for that. Much to the contrary. Similarly, Kimberly Lowelle, president of The Labyrinth Society, a network of labyrinth scholars and enthusiasts, writes, "The labyrinth is an archetype of transformation. Its transcendent nature knows no boundaries, crossing time and cultures with ease. The labyrinth serves as a bridge from the mundane to the divine."[63]

Perhaps Lowelle means this metaphorically. But perhaps she doesn't. And therein lies the danger—one person could see "the bridge" as metaphoric, and another could take Lowelle's words literally. God's Word clearly indicates that while there is "a bridge from the mundane to the divine," there is only one—and it's not the labyrinth. First Timothy 2:5-6 shuts that door when it says, "For there is one God, and there is one mediator between God and men, the man Christ Jesus, who gave himself as a ransom for all."

My point is that too many Evangelicals are adopting practices they believe will enhance their spiritual growth, yet those practices have a history of doing everything except enhancing spiritual growth. Walking the labyrinth appears to fall into this category.

Someone may say, "But I don't walk the labyrinth for anything but to draw closer to God in prayer." I'll accept that. A biblically-minded person such as Dan Kimball might use the practice only for good, but let's not be naïve. Walking the labyrinth has not always been used for biblical purposes, nor does it predominantly continue to be used for biblical purposes today.

A final "spiritual discipline" that needs a word or two of caution is the practice of *lectio divina.* Wait a minute! What could possibly be wrong with *lectio divina*? Maybe nothing. But before we adopt or even adapt any practice, we should know its origins and what we are getting ourselves in to.

Practice #4: *Lectio Divina*

Lectio divina is Latin for "divine reading." It refers to an ancient practice of praying the Scriptures. During *lectio divina* it is claimed that the practitioner listens to the text of the Bible with an "ear of the heart." The purpose of reading the Bible with the heart, say practitioners, is to enter into a conversation with God where God suggests the topics for discussion. I would rather that practitioners emphasize reading the Bible with both heart and mind as the Bible itself suggests.

In its purest sense, I endorse the concept of *lectio divina* because it is the lack of Bible engagement that has caused many of the problems in the Church today, and *lectio divina* gets people involved with Scripture. So there are many good things to be said about this practice, but let's investigate it with eyes wide open.

> **"Perhaps the reason *lectio divina* has become such a hit with Evangelicals in the last couple of decades is because this is what we should have been doing all along."**

Monastic Origins

Lectio divina is an integral part of the Roman Catholic tradition, specifically in the Benedictine and Cistercian monastic traditions. The original practice existed with the simple attentive reading of Scripture or commentaries by the early Fathers of the Church, but it has expanded far beyond that today. *Lectio divina* is firmly rooted within the Christian monastic and contemplative heritage. By the time of St. Benedict in the 6th century it had already become a regular practice within monasteries. As often is the case with subjective and experiential practices, *lectio divina* has evolved into several forms, but with most forms of the practice, there are four basic steps:

1. **Reading** *(lectio)* requires reading the Bible passage gently and slowly several times. The passage itself is not as important as the savoring of each portion of the reading, constantly listening for the "still, small voice" of a word or phrase that somehow speaks to the person reading.
2. **Reflecting** *(meditatio)* means reflecting on the text of the passage being read and thinking about how it applies to life. This is a very personal reading of the Scripture in which a person searches for a very personal application.
3. **Responding** *(oratio)* to the passage being read is done by opening our hearts to the heart to God. This is not primarily an intellectual exercise, but is more of the beginning of a silent conversation with God.
4. **Resting** *(contemplatio)* is contemplation, listening silently to God. This involves freeing ourselves of our own thoughts, whatever they may be, and

emptying our minds to receive what God has to say to us. It is described as opening the mind, heart, and soul to the influence of God.

None of these four basic steps is unbiblical. In fact, perhaps the reason *lectio divina* has become such a hit with Evangelicals in the last couple of decades is because this is what we should have been doing all along—reading and reflecting on God's Word, responding to His message, and contemplating what that means for our walk as Christ-followers. These practices have always been a part of the biblical plan for spiritual growth.

There would be no reason to express concerns about the practice of *lectio divina* if these four steps were all that was meant by those who use the term or champion it. But, unfortunately, the practice of *lectio divina* comes with some historical baggage. So we must dig deeper to discern whether this practice is worthwhile or not.

Good intentions, questionable theology

I mentioned that *lectio divina* traces its roots to Roman Catholic tradition, particularly in the Benedictine order. Specifically, the concept of reading Scripture and meditating on it comes directly from the 48th chapter of the *Rule of St. Benedict* (AD 480-453), a book written by Benedict to guide monastic life and the standard text for Benedictine monastics.

Lectio divina was not formalized until the 11th century when a Carthusian prior named Guigo (AD 1083-1136) described the practice in a letter to a brother monk. In that letter, (which has come to be known as *Scala Paradisi),* Guigo describes *lectio divina* as a four-runged ladder to heaven. He wrote that by practicing these four steps in *lectio divina,* one is actually climbing the stairway to heaven. Salvation comes, according to Guigo, by the self-effort of practicing *lectio divina.* Guigo even names the four-runged ladder to heaven as *lectio, meditatio, oratio,* and *contemplatio.*

The point here is that historically, the emphasis of *lectio divina* hasn't been on the message of the Bible *per se*, but on the process or the way the Bible is read as a means unto salvation. Indeed, Guigo claimed that the methodology led to heaven.

Lengthening the ladder

Later Catholic tradition added three more steps to the original four, making salvation even more the result of works than a matter of grace. The steps became:

1. *statio* (position)
2. *lectio* (reading)
3. *meditatio* (meditation)
4. *oratio* (prayer)
5. *contemplatio* (contemplation)
6. *collation* (discussion)
7. *actio* (action)

One author describes how a proper position is conducive to a deepened relationship with God. He writes:

"First, we arrange a place so it is restful, warm, and non-distracting. This may involve the lighting of candles, the burning of incense, the shutting of doors and drawing of curtains—whatever makes one feel calm and at peace. Then we assume a bodily posture that is conducive to prayer and reading. We breathe slowly, focusing on the Holy Name of Jesus and nothing else, until we are relaxed and able to focus our attention solely on Scripture. If our minds wander, we gently bring our attention back to the Holy Name of Our Lord, breathing in and out rhythmically. . . The presence of relevant icons and other visual aids to meditation can be of great benefit."[64]

The writer concludes with an admonition to parents regarding the family, "Make the Bible a familiar and integral part of their lives."

At first glance, who can argue with that? I've been preaching that myself for decades. Care needs to be taken to read the Bible carefully and reverently, and the Bible needs to be a familiar and integral part of family life. That's the whole point of Deuteronomy 6:5-9.

But we can't help but be wary when a writer discusses the *process* of reading Scriptures in much detail without ever pointing readers to the greater importance of the *meaning* of Scripture itself. Did you catch that omission? Within this writer's description, his omission speaks volumes. Unfortunately, for some who practice *lectio divina*, they allow procedure and process to rob them of genuinely hearing from God.

If you think I'm being overly concerned about this, please note that this same author continues: "A partial indulgence is granted to the faithful, who, under the usual conditions and with the veneration due the divine word, make a spiritual reading from Sacred Scripture. A plenary indulgence is granted under the usual conditions if this reading is continued for at least one half an hour."[65]

Say what?

I think I hear Martin Luther turning over in his grave.

Suddenly what should be a beautiful thing has become a means to earn your way to heaven. That's not only bad theology it's also bad for the practice of *lectio divina*. Before the Evangelical church completely embraces what sounds like a wonderful way to read God's Word, we should be aware of the deep-seeded concept of works-righteousness from which *lectio divina* has sprouted. Paul insisted in Ephesians 2:8-10 that grace is a gift of God, and not a result of works.

> *"Suddenly what should be a beautiful thing has become a means to earn our way to heaven."*

So, yes, some of the spiritual formation movement that finds its roots in Roman Catholicism is tainted with the inbred concept that spiritual formation is a way to work our way to God. That doesn't mean we can't cut away some of the weeds from this garden and benefit from its fruit and vegetables, but it does mean we have to engage God's Word consistently and understand it as the Holy Spirit intended or else we will adopt without discernment what means something significantly different from what we thought.

At the end of the day, *lectio divina* can be a marvelous thing. The concepts of reading, reflecting, responding, and resting can be very helpful in our spiritual journey to the heart of God. But to take complete advantage of these concepts, we must rid them of the excess baggage they bring. We must pull weeds from the garden, strip tradition from truth, and find true biblical validation for how we seek to know God better. If we do that, *lectio divina* could be an aide to our spiritual growth and not an adversary. If we don't do it, *lectio divina* will become just another entrée on the spiritual salad bar.

A better and proven way

In conclusion, these are spiritual formation programs and practices that offer a mixed bag of blessings. But there is a better and proven way to grow close to the Lord. It's His way, His chosen method of deepening our relationship with Him and growing in Christ. That's engaging the Bible by reading His Word, soundly studying Scripture with both mind and heart, allowing the Holy Spirit of God to mold us into the image of Christ, and living out God's principles in action. If you want to grow spiritually and move down the road toward spiritual maturity, that's where you should place the bulk of your attention.

There's not a lot of jazz in this solution, but there is a lot of truth. And, even more to the point, while many supposed spiritual formation practices hope to contribute to your spiritual growth, only one practice can be proven scientifically to do so and that is the consistent, meaningful engagement in God's Word.

If you want to grow spiritually, engage God through His Word.

CHAPTER 14

Benching Your Star Quarterback

God is very clear. He has not been silent; He has spoken and He wants you to know and understand what He has said. In fact, He wants you not only to know and understand, He wants to help you live by what He said in a way that pleases Him and benefits you. But we so often miss God's best for us because we get bogged down in the everyday cares of life or in ineffective ways of trying to get to know God.

As we have just seen, there are numerous spiritual disciplines that clamor for our attention today. Many of them are legitimate, biblical and very useful. Some may appear to be biblical because they sound so spiritual, but they have roots in places other than the Bible.

The point I want to make here is that engaging God's Word consistently is not just one of the spiritual disciplines; it is the primary spiritual discipline. I am not just paying the obligatory respect for God's Word. I am saying that engaging God by engaging His Word in a meaningful, life-changing way stands head and shoulders above all the other disciplines. *Prima scriptura*, the Bible first, the Bible above all, is the sure path that God has chosen for you. It is not on an equal footing with all the others, as it is often presented to be in books on the spiritual disciplines; the Bible isn't even first among equals. It has no equal. God only wrote one book and I think He'd be pleased to have us read it. This is the sure path to spiritual maturity; it is God's path.

But we have choices. We can ignore the sure path. We can add other paths and give them equal time with God's unique Word. Or, we can identify the road-blocks that keep us from the sure path, remove them and find a way to make real progress down the road toward spiritual maturity.

Going with your star

Picture this. You're a college football coach. Your star quarterback has every play in his head or inscribed on his arm band. He has weathered game after game, season after season and has never lost a game. He hasn't even thrown an interception in his entire college career. Yes he has a back, a tight end, a wide-out and others who contribute to the game, but he's the key. Without him, your team is nothing. And even though you know that the other players together can't make you a winner, you bench your quarterback and look to the others to carry the load. Is that good coaching? Is it the way to win? Of course not, yet within Christianity many have benched the Bible in their pursuit of spiritual maturity. They have placed on the sidelines of their spiritual formation game plan the only player that can bring them victory.

> *"The Bible is respected, but not heeded. It is revered, but not read. It is viewed as God's Word, but disregarded as the standard of Christian belief and behavior."*

There are two words that describe how people today view the Bible: respect and disregard. That may sound oxymoronic, but let me explain. For most Christians, the Bible continues to hold a place of admiration and respect. Sources say [66] the three top-selling books of all time (to date) are the Harry Potter series (approximately 400 million copies), the *Thoughts of Chairman Mao* (800-900 million copies) and the Bible (2.5 billion copies). Other estimates put copies of the Bible sold as high as 6 billion. [67] By any calculation, the Bible is still the world's best seller.

Not only do Christians continue to buy Bibles, for the most part they continue to respect them. While this respect is sometimes not displayed in governmental, educational or legal venues, the Bible continues to hold a place of reverence in homes, churches and various institutions.

Reverence does not equate to reading

This reverence, however, has taken a strange twist in recent decades. The Bible is respected, but not heeded. It is revered, but not read. It is viewed as God's Word, but disregarded as the standard of Christian belief and behavior.

The Barna Group recently surveyed Christians on what areas of their faith development they were most confident about, and what areas needed work. Christians felt confident that their interpersonal relationships were going smoothly overall, as well as their ability to worship. However when respondents were asked to identify the aspect of their faith that needed the most improvement, their two most common responses were a need to commit more strongly to their faith, and to increase their knowledge of the Bible. [68] Barna noted, "The data show that millions of people who are aligned with the Christian faith have not thought very much or very clearly about what spiritual maturity means."[69]

A Princeton Religion Research Center's study entitled *The Bible and the American People* indicated that "while the frequency of Bible reading appears to have changed only slightly over recent decades, belief *about* the Bible has changed dramatically. Biblical literalism—the belief that the Bible represents the actual word of God—has declined over these decades, and is now at the lowest point ever recorded (27 percent). In 1963, the comparable figure was 65 percent."[70]

The facts speak for themselves.

Reverence does not equate to belief

In another Barna survey, when given thirteen basic teachings from the Bible, only 1 percent of adult believers firmly embraced all thirteen as being biblical perspectives.[71] One out of thirteen!

Author David Wells summarized this trend: "I have watched with growing disbelief as the Evangelical church has cheerfully plunged into astounding theological illiteracy."[72]

This marginalization of the Bible has paved the way for non-biblical beliefs and practices to make their way into mainstream Christianity. In preparing to write this book I have read more than 50 books on spiritual formation. Some are classics; others are destined to languish on the dusty bookshelves of obscure libraries. In many respects, I have read one book fifty times because most books on spiritual formation say pretty much the same thing. They advocate very much the same spiritual disciplines. They come almost to the same conclusions.

What I find both interesting and disheartening in the literature on spiritual formation is the quick and easy dismissal of the Bible from the discussion. Few writing on the subject dismiss the Bible outright. That would be theological suicide. In fact, many begin with the importance of Bible reading and especially Bible meditation, but quickly move to subjects the writers obviously appear to find more helpful: solitude, centering prayer, reading the Desert Fathers and a host of biblically-unrelated topics.

It is this Bible marginalization that I believe flaws much of today's discussion on spiritual formation. Whether intentional or not, the Bible is often speedily dismissed as the centerpiece for engaging God in a meaningful way.

Bible Marginalization Seeps Into Church Leadership

What's equally problematic is that some mainline Evangelical leaders follow this trend, and openly marginalize the place of the Bible in spiritual formation. I recently attended two large-scale Evangelical gatherings where this took place. These leaders, I believe, are well meaning. They make the point that it takes more than sheer Bible knowledge to grow spiritually. I heartily agree. I've said that over and over in this book. They want to ensure that Evangelical churches don't evaluate spirituality maturity solely on the basis of how well a person can identify Bible characters, interpret Bible passages, quote Bible verses, and explain biblical theology. I see their point—the ability to debate doctrine is considered by some as the ultimate proof of a person's spirituality, and this should not be.

But I would argue that those messages come across as too eager to marginalize the importance of the Bible. Pushed slightly, the messages say that if a person teaches Bible content and doctrine, it has a debilitating effect on spiritual growth. On that I strenuously disagree. Rather, it is the *lack* of teaching Bible content and doctrine that has been proven to cause severe retardation of spiritual growth among Christians.

Are we over-committed to the Bible?

In another talk a few years back, a well-known professor at a solid Evangelical seminary contended that within the practices of the Evangelical community in North America, there has been an over-commitment to Scripture in a way that is false, irrational, and even harmful to the cause of Christ. This over-commitment has produced a mean-spiritedness among the over-committed, said the speaker, that "is a grotesque and often ignorant distortion of discipleship unto the Lord Jesus." He has a point about mean-spirited Christians, but I think God would have cause to question our being "over-committed" to Scripture.

Ted Olsen rebutted the speaker in an article in *Christianity Today.* He wrote, with sheer incredulity: "To accuse evangelicals of over-commitment to the Bible [at the Evangelical Theological Society], is like accusing environmentalists of talking too much about climate change at a Sierra Club meeting."[73]

Please understand that I don't believe any of my Evangelical colleagues have lowered their view of Scripture. But when a speaker marginalizes Scripture, it doesn't deny the validity of the Bible, it just dethrones the supremacy of it. With all the other spiritual disciplines being touted today, to marginalize the importance of the Bible in spiritual formation is like benching your star quarterback during a bowl game and replacing him with a red-shirt freshman. No coach in his right mind would do that, and yet Christians, even prominent leaders within the Church, are doing the spiritual equivalent all the time.

The key to Bible engagement

Unless we have the Bible as our main course, we will always be hungry for more solid food. Yet perhaps the Bible has been so conspicuously absent in the spiritual formation discussion because of the approach we have adopted to the Bible. I will concede that.

For example, some read the Bible to discover truth. That's good. Passages such Ephesians 1:13 and 2 Timothy 2:15 indicate that the Bible is the source of divine truth. But reading the Bible simply to discover truth doesn't necessarily help a person engage with the Author.

Others read the Bible to find comfort. Passages such as Psalm 23 and Isaiah 40 are wonderful places to be reminded of God's comfort, hope and encouragement. Reading those passages might help a person feel better, but he or she may not have actually interacted with God during those readings.

Still others make it their practice to read the Bible to unearth answers to questions. The word "why" occurs more than 275 times in the Bible. If you want answers, the Bible is the best place to go. But even in acquiring answers to their questions, a person may have ignored the Book's author.

Read to discover God

The real solution is to approach the Bible as the divinely-ordained, God-chosen method of engaging God. When we read the Bible, we have the ability to discover God. We can connect with God, hear from God, and enter into divine correspondence with Him. The Bible is where we discover intimacy with God, because the Bible is God's choice to communicate with us and reveal Himself to us.

To know God isn't a process of emptying our minds or centering ourselves; it involves a process of filling ourselves with His Word and centering ourselves on Him. We know we have experienced God when we have genuinely engaged Him in the Scriptures that came from His heart and mind.

If you are unfulfilled in your relationship with God, if you don't seem to be making any headway on the road to spiritual maturity, if you are pretty much spiritually where you were the day after your salvation, there's something wrong. The problem isn't with God's Word or His plan for our spiritual formation. The problem is that we often marginalize God's Word or find ourselves too busy to meaningfully engage the Bible on a consistent basis. We wouldn't put up with one meal a week on our table, but many Christians are fine with one meal from God's Word every Sunday morning. That's benching the quarterback and it may be the reason they are losing the game.

Spiritual formation without significant interaction with God's Word ends up being little more than smoke and mirrors. The key to spiritual growth is unquestionably our growing intimacy with God as gained through quality and quantity time in His Word.

As A.W. Tozer said, "God is in this Book . . . and if you want to find Him, go into this Book."[74]

CHAPTER 15

"Start Your Engines"—It's Time to Roll

Throughout the pages of this book I have advocated that you adopt engaging the Bible as the quintessential tool to produce spiritual maturity in your life. I hope I have given you some things to think about. The Bible is God's roadmap to spiritual maturity, His instruction manual for spiritual formation, His heavenly GPS, the revelation of God that explains by precept and example how to become more intimate with Him.

But it's one thing to *talk* about reading God's Word. It's quite another to actually *do* it. Paradoxically, the main objective I've had for you is hurry up and finish this book, put it aside, so you can pick up God's Book—your Bible—and read that! That's where you'll learn about spiritual formation.

Now, I know that much of what you've read has been surprising to you but I want to conclude by being as helpful to you as I can be. I want this chapter to be as practical as I can make it. If you're beginning to think you may have been on the wrong path, you may have gotten sidetracked in the cul-de-sac of mystical spiritual practices and you want to get some traction on the road to spiritual maturity, this chapter is for you. It's down-to-earth stuff. It's time to get on the sure path to spiritual formation, the path that both the Bible advocates and a growing body of scientific evidence indicates is the right path—God's path. I want you to discover a book that perhaps you have thought was too imposing for you to pick up and read.

So, for all you NASCAR fans, "Gentlemen (and Ladies), start your engines." It's time to for you to get going, so let's exam in some depth two foundational, yet often overlooked questions: *why* people should read the Bible, and *how* people should read the Bible? These questions may sound basic, but I've purposely placed this chapter at the end of this book in preparation for what I really want you to do—read your Bible! I don't mean to suggest that you haven't been reading the Bible all along this journey. But I hope you have a new sense of urgency and expectancy in the process. God is waiting to be discovered in the pages of His Word. His has revealed a lot of things in His Word that you may not yet have made a part of your life. You've skipped over them or you've been inconsistent in encountering them. So let's take a look at those two basic questions. First, the *why* question.

Why should I read my Bible?

The Bible itself offers at least ten specific reasons why you should read it. Consider them with me.
Read your Bible because:

1. **God's Word is not just any ordinary book**. Hebrews 4:12, "For the word of God is living and active, sharper than any two-edged sword, piercing to the division of soul and of spirit, of joints and of marrow, and discerning the thoughts and intentions of the heart."
2. **God's Word is the necessary ingredient for spiritual formation**. Acts 20:32, "And now I commend you to God and to the word of his grace, which is able to build you up and to give you the inheritance among all those who are sanctified."
3. **God's Word is a genuine source of encouragement in a world without hope.** Romans 15:4, "For whatever was written in former days was written for our instruction, that through endurance and through the encouragement of the Scriptures we might have hope."
4. **God's Word is the safeguard against sin.** Psalm 119:11, "I have stored up your word in my heart, that I might not sin against you."
5. **God's Word sets people free.** John 8:31-32, "So Jesus said to the Jews who had believed in him, 'If you abide in my word, you are truly my disciples, and you will know the truth, and the truth will set you free.'"
6. **God's Word shows the pathway to true success.** Joshua 1:8, "This book of the Law shall not depart from your mouth, but you shall meditate on it day and night, so that you may be careful to do according to all that is written in it. For then you will make your way prosperous, and then you will have good success."
7. **God's Word is our training manual for successful service**. 2 Timothy 3:16-17, "All Scripture is breathed out by God and profitable for teaching, for reproof, for correction, and for training in righteousness, that the man of God may be competent, equipped for every good work."
8. **God's Word provides essential nourishment for spiritual life.** John 6:63, "The words that I have spoken to you are spirit and life."
9. **God's Word is the core of Christian life.** John 14:23-24, "If anyone loves me, he will keep my word, and my Father will love him, and we will come

to him and make our home with him. Whoever does not love me does not keep my words."

10. **God's Word is the necessary ingredient for life itself.** Matthew 4:4, "Man shall not live by bread alone, but by every word that comes from the mouth of God."

There are many more reasons, of course, but these show that the Bible is not lacking in specific encouragement for you to read it. I have not tried to change them or dress them up because every born-again person has the Spirit of God residing in him or her and you don't need me to teach you these things; you only need to be reminded of them (2 Peter 3:1-2).

Why people don't read their Bible

I am often asked if people should read the whole Bible, and my answer is always yes. 2 Timothy 3:16 says that "All Scripture is God-breathed and is useful for teaching, rebuking, correcting, and training in righteousness." The key word in that verse is "all." Not "some" or "most." It's all. All Scripture is useful. But a lot of people jump around in their reading of God's Word and become frustrated so they just set it aside and forget about it.

Researchers at The Center for Bible Engagement wondered what reasons people give for not reading their Bibles. So the CBE asked them. They surveyed 40,000 Americans ranging from eight years of age to more than 80. Surveys included both random samples of the general population and non-random samples of self-identified Christ-followers. To get the most complete picture possible, CBE researchers included a mix of both close-ended and open-ended questions. People were given enough space to answer the questions with a few words or a few sentences. The point was to allow people to be honest, to tell the research team exactly what kept them from reading God's Word, and did they ever tell the CBE. Their findings showed that, contrary to spiritual urban legends, people don't see the Bible as being irrelevant or boring. In fact, 1.6 percent of respondents gave "not a priority" as the reason why they don't read the Bible. Another 0.4 percent said "lack of motivation." Are you surprised? Be honest, didn't you assume most people don't read their Bible because they thought it was not relevant to modern life or because they said it was just too boring. Not so.

Overwhelmingly people admitted they don't read their Bible because they see it as being time-consuming.

I don't have time

The number one reason why people say they do not read the Bible is, "I don't have time." Of those responding to the CBE survey, a whopping 51.2 percent gave "too busy" as the reason for not reading the Bible. The next closest reason ("too distracted") garnered a measly 6.8% of respondents and the numbers went straight downhill from there.

This no-time excuse made me curious. So I set out to find out how much time it actually takes to read the entire Bible cover to cover. Over the course of several months, every free hour I had, every plane trip I took, every moment of down time, I read my Bible and timed myself as I read it. I literally hung a stopwatch around my neck like a football coach and set out to time how long it took to read every book in the Bible.

Now, I don't suggest you do this. If people simply mark off days on a Bible reading guide with an attitude of getting a day behind them, that's not the way to become spiritually mature through the Word. We need some soaking-in time when we read the Bible. But my purpose was simply to find out if the "I don't have time" excuse is actually valid. My conclusion was that it is clearly not.

Without speed reading, at a leisurely pace, and clicking my stopwatch to pause every time I was interrupted and then clicking it again as I returned to read, I was able to read the entire Bible in fewer than 72 hours. In fact, half the books of the Bible I could read in less than 30 minutes each; 26 of them in less than 15 minutes each. It seems astounding to me that a person can live for years and still use the "I don't have time" excuse to justify why they have never read the only book God ever wrote. Let's be honest. Time isn't the problem; desire is. We basically do what we want to do. We find the time for whatever is important to us. If reading God's Word is important to you, you'll find the time; if it isn't, you won't. I hate being so blunt, but it's the truth and we all know it.

My challenge to you is to read your Bible—the entire Bible—because it is where God has chosen to speak to you, to reveal His mind to you, and to let you in on the nuances of His character that cannot be known through nature or conscience. You can do it: God will help.

> *"The Bible is respected, but not heeded. It is revered, but not read. It is viewed as God's Word, but disregarded as the standard of Christian belief and behavior."*

The Bible is difficult to understand

In the CBE survey others claimed they didn't read their Bible because they found it too difficult to understand. While just a small percentage of respondents opted for this reason (only 0.8 percent), nevertheless it must be admitted that some portions of God's Word are more difficult to read and understand than others. Even after 2,000 years of Church history, some Bible passages and teachings leave the most accomplished Bible scholars scratching their heads. I know they do me.

It's not because God lacked the communicative skills necessary to make the message clear and plain. The message of God's Word is perfectly clear. The more a person reads the Bible the more clearly he or she sees that message. But there are several valid and understandable reasons why we sometimes have difficulty understanding the Bible.

Clouded ability to understand

For one thing, we are fallen creatures, people stained with sin living among others stained with sin. As Isaiah the prophet said, "Woe is me! For I am lost; for I am a man of unclean lips, and I dwell in the midst of a people of unclean lips" (Isaiah 6:5). Sin can cloud our thinking and block our ability to understand the Bible.

Varied literary genre

Another reason why we sometimes have difficulty in understanding the Bible is that the books of the Bible are not all of the same type. Some books are prophecy, others are personal letters. Some books are poetry, others are history. Some books make frequent use of symbolism, parables or allegories; others just report the facts. If we aren't prepared to understand the books in the genre in which they were written, we are ill-prepared to understand the Bible. Again, we need to let the Bible say what it wants to, in the way it wants to say it.

Cultural differences

One of the most common reasons we may have difficulty understanding the Bible is cultural. The Bible was written between 2,000 and 4,000 years ago. That's a long time. And while that has no bearing at all on its accuracy, it certainly bears on its understandability. The cultural differences between us today and those who lived in Bible times are enormous. We drive a Camaro; they drove a camel. We write on an iPad; they wrote on papyrus. The cultural differences between our two societies naturally cause some difficulties in understanding. Can you picture Moses leading the children of Israel through the wilderness with a GPS duct-taped to his staff? (I wonder if he would have asked his wife Zipporah for directions.).

But differences in culture do not change the meaning of the text or the morality it conveys. Truth is still truth whether it's recorded in 1400 B.C. or A.D. 2012. God wants us to become familiar with Him. He wants us to enjoy Him. He wants us to be intimate with Him, and even though we may have to wade through a difficult passage here or there, we can do it. God can help. He gives us the Holy Spirit to teach us all the things we need to know. (John 14:16, 18, 25-27).

The "how" question

How should we read the Bible?

I believe God's call on my life is to help those stuck in spiritual infancy to move toward spiritual maturity. After half a century of ministry, I've learned that a person can't make any progress if he or she isn't willing to pick up God's Word and read it—consistently, meaningfully. So the question emerges this way, "I know I need to read my Bible—but how do I begin, where do I begin, when do I begin?"

Here's how to get going:

1. **Get the right spirit.**

If you want to get the most out of your Bible reading, you need a little preparation—of yourself. The best way to accomplish this is to enlist superior help. Before you begin reading, take a few minutes to pray and ask the Holy Spirit of God to assist you in understanding what you read.

Here are four prayers I typically ask of the Holy Spirit to help me with before I read the Bible:

   a. *A prayer to take out the trash.* I ask God to cleanse me from all sin. Nothing hinders us from getting to know the heart and mind of God like personal sin. I lay the things I know stand between me and intimacy with God out there, name them, admit them, and agree with God that I need to be cleansed from them to get the most out of reading the Bible (1 John 1:9).

   b. *A prayer to focus on God.* Once I have "taken out the trash," I ask the Holy Spirit to fill that void with Himself and His Word. Specifically, I ask Him to help me get the point of what the writer wanted to convey to me. I ask the Spirit to keep my mind from rabbit trails, from that "deer in the headlights" look that can come when zoned out, and from allowing the challenges of my day to creep into my mind while reading.

c. *A prayer for insight.* I ask God to give me spiritual insight that I do not natu-rally possess. Within this prayer, I ask Him to keep me from error, personal bias, personal agendas, and personal hobby horses. I ask Him to show me truth, regardless of what I believed before.

d. *A prayer for life change.* I ask Him to cement what I learn from the Bible in my heart and mind, and ask Him to show me how to use what I learn by engaging God's Word in my life this day. I ask Him to take what I read and make a difference in my life, to help move me down the road toward spiritual maturity.

These prayers are not like peeling away the false self to get to the real self or centering down to the core of my spiritual being to find God. They are requests to the Living God to help me understand and act based on what the Sovereign God has already revealed to me in His Holy Word.

2. **Get the right stuff.**

By "right stuff," I'm talking about reading God's Word intentionally to become "competent, equipped for every good work" (2 Timothy 3:17). This is not a hap-hazard process of flipping open the Bible and reading whatever catches your eye. But rather a serious and disciplined process where you give time, attention, and focus to God's Word.

Bible reading can become a great adventure of learning about God and your-self. Pragmatically, the right stuff consists of the three important tools:

a. *The right Bible.* You need to become familiar and comfortable with your personal Bible. I always encourage people to get a translation they will read and understand—one that preserves the majesty of God's Word without hiding that majesty in archaic language and difficult-to-understand language. When asked, "What's the best Bible translation?" I always respond, "The one you read."

b. *The right method of recording what you learn* and the impressions the Spirit of God burns into your mind. The old Chinese proverb is correct: "The faintest ink is more powerful than the strongest memory." Since much of your power of memory depends on what you write down, I always recommend that people study the Bible as they hold something to write with (such as a pen or pencil) and something to write on (such as a notebook, iPad, or laptop). Tremendous meaning is found when you jot down personal insights and truths you have discovered for yourself while reading God's Word.

c. *The right storage system* for remembering what you read. I encourage people to make their own categories or lists of things from reading the Bible. It's surprising how often you encounter the same theme or issue in the Bible. In various folders within my laptop I have categories for a variety of things, such as every time God gives a double call, everyone who said "I have sinned" (that's quite a list), the great questions posed in the Bible, interesting names of people, names of unimpressive people, sad verses in the Bible, references to money or riches, the "I Am" passages, every time the Bible says "the battle is the Lord's", twins in the Bible, actual letters recorded in the Bible, great prayers of the Bible, verses that are especially convicting to me, and much more. You might say, "Well that's fine for you, but those things don't interest me." That's just the point. Make your own list of things that are meaningful to you.

For maximum personal benefit to you as you read God's Word you need to prepare yourself and your environment. Make engaging God's Word as meaningful to you as it can be by making your environment and you as ready to receive from God whatever He wants to reveal to you.

3. **Get the right space.**

By "space" I mean develop a place that contributes to a significant connection with God. My wife and I live in the country on a five-acre plot of land. We have plenty of space. Now that the kids are grown and gone, she would say we have too much space. But when we were first married we rented two rooms on the top floor of an elderly widow's home. We shared our landlady's kitchen downstairs along with her refrigerator (she had two shelves and we had two shelves—she often liked our food better, so we shared that too). How much space you have is immaterial; that you find a space and get the right space to meet with God is critical.

There are three important findings essential to getting the right space.

a. *Find a quiet space.* When you meet with God, you need to do so in a space where you will not be disturbed. We live in a multi-tasking world and we are proud of it. We can text, drive, unwrap a Big Mac and put on make-up all while we reprogram the GPS in our car. These habits often bleed into our time with God. People jog and pray, ride a stationary bike and pray, read the Bible and watch the news at the same time. But when Jesus wanted to engage His Heavenly Father in a meaningful way, He got alone, in a remote place where He would find a quiet space (Matthew 14:23; Mark 6:45-47;

Luke 9:18; John 6:15). Jesus' pattern can teach you much about how to enhance your intimacy with the Father.

b. *Find a comfortable space.* By this I don't mean an easy chair in which you can recline and possibly fall asleep while reading. I mean a place where you feel "comfortable," a place where you feel non-threatened, where you can stay for hours if you choose, a place where you can be intimate with God without embarrassment. Of course, you can engage God through His Word anywhere, but your deepest, most intimate engagement will come in that place where you are most comfortable with Him.

c. *Find a consistent place.* This needs to be the space where you can go back time after time, day after day, and meet God there. It's a place that becomes familiar to you and where you can feel the presence of God. When I was in college I was a language major. Don't ask me why, but I studied French, German, Spanish, Latin, Greek and Hebrew—all at the same time. I continued the study of four of these languages in seminary. At that time Linda and I, and our two oldest children who were three and two years old, lived in a mobile home. She worked full time, I worked full time, and I went to seminary full time. I needed to find the right space to learn these languages and continue my seminary studies. So I chose a different spot for each language, such as a chair in the living room, a desk in the bedroom, the kitchen table, etc., and always returned to that space and studied only one language at each space. When I took exams in those languages, I would mentally transport myself back to that space where things became familiar to me and that helped me to keep the languages separated. That was a good lesson to me about meeting with God. It's always been helpful to me to find a consistent, quiet, comfortable space. Throughout my day I can transport myself mentally back to that place. There's nothing mystical here, it's all practical. Try it. It will work for you too.

4. **Get the right strategy.**

The right strategy is an individual strategy, a strategy that works for you. Your intent is to read the only book God ever wrote and to encounter Him there in a way that moves you on to spiritual maturity. How will you do that?

A less than strategic approach to spiritual growth will lead to diminished spiritual growth. So I always encourage people that they need a game plan to get from A to Z spiritually. Will it be a chapter a day? Perhaps read one chapter from the Old Testament, one from the New Testament, and one Psalm each day? Maybe it's one book of the Bible at a time, perhaps even in one sitting. Will it be a morning-only strategy or a morning- and evening- strategy? It's okay to use the strategies of others.

Some years ago I developed a dozen "reading plans" which we have offered free online through our ministry's website. I wanted to provide a reading strategy that would fit various harried lifestyles, so I devised a morning and evening guide, a chronological reading guide, a two-year reading guide (for those who need some extra time reading through the Bible), a weekend guide (for those who said they didn't have opportunity to read on workdays), a blended guide (which pared similar themes in the Old Testament with the New Testament), and more.

Researchers at The Center for Bible Engagement have discovered that most new Bible readers do not benefit from a Bible reading guide, but more mature Christians do. There may be a level of spiritual maturity that has to be achieved before an aggressive "through the Bible" strategy becomes effective. When people are beginners, I recommend developing a strategy that moves them to that place in their spiritual formation where the consistent, strategic reading of God's Word becomes a necessary habit of life. If you're new at this, bite off smaller bits at a time and adopt a strategy that helps you move incrementally down the road to spiritual maturity.

Most of life doesn't just happen. It is planned and then pursued. Spiritual forma-tion is the same way. If you get the right strategy for encountering God, you'll be successful. But if you fail to get the right strategy, you will likely fail in your pursuit of spiritual formation. Find a strategy that is the right fit for you. Experiment. There is no one-size-fits-all. Develop your own or borrow from others and adapt their strategy for your personal needs.

5. **Get the right significance.**

Have you ever worked long days into short nights and finally discovered that all your efforts brought you to wrong conclusions and your work vanished into thin air? If you've had that painful experience, you can identify with getting the right significance. It's like leaning your ladder on the wrong wall or painting the wrong house. Great effort; poor results.

The Bible has an unveiling plan of God's redemption. It is not compartmental-ized, but it is fluid. Reading through the Bible helps you to get the significance of why God does what He does, at the times He does them. It's called progressive revelation. The deeper into God's Word you get, the deeper into His mind you get. The farther along God's Word you read, the farther along your understanding of His love for you, His plans and promises for you, His intentions for you. Remember, the Bible is a revelation of the mind of God to the minds of men. You haven't gotten the right significance out of God's Word until you can "read His mind."

While some authors say that the *right* issues I've just talked about are secondary and not important, you are wise enough to know that it's often "the little foxes that spoil the vineyards" (Song of Solomon 2:15), in other words—secondary things can defeat a primary purpose. Success comes in paying attention to the details. Getting it right isn't brain surgery. You don't have to be a rocket scientist to get it right. You just need to use good, common, spiritual sense.

And you can do it! God will help.

CONCLUSION

One Final Thought

I have good news. There is great hope ahead. Surely we must consider it a positive sign that people are searching for spirituality with greater fervency than in decades past. People are hearing the calling of God in their souls. They're listening to the echoes of His glory, bouncing around in the God-shaped hole in their hearts, and they're seeking rest for their hearts, the kind of rest that can only be found in Jesus Christ. While not all are seeking for spiritual fulfillment in the right places, it is still a good sign that they are seeking for spiritual fulfillment.

If I could leave you with just one thought at the close of this book, it would be this: according to the Bible itself and a growing body of scientific research, the key to transformation from spiritual immaturity to spiritual maturity is found exclusively in a growing intimacy with God through His Word. Many of the techniques of the new Christian spirituality are attractive, even sensational, but many also smack more of Eastern mysticism than biblical Christianity. Yet, growing numbers of Christians have bought into them without knowing their connections to false religions or the spiritual baggage they bring with them. Don't be fooled by the new items on the spiritual salad bar. The presentation is great; the nutritional value—not so much.

The on-going transformation in the Christian life

Transformation is a key concept in Christian thinking. The greatest transformation comes at the moment of our salvation, when as sinners walking in darkness we are transformed into saints walking in the light (John 8:12). But while at the moment of salvation we pass from death into life (John 5:24; 1 John 3:14), transformation continues throughout our Christian life, for life itself requires transformation. In the physical realm we are born babies but we grow into adults. That's transformation. And that's the same kind of transformation we should expect to see in our spiritual lives.

Leaders of the church today are increasingly seeing the need to read the Bible for transformation, not just for information. But while much is being made over the need for transformation, (not just biblical information), I would argue that current research shows that Christians are not so much being filled with information which they are failing to transform. Rather, Christians aren't filled with enough information to begin with. The real issue—one which fewer appear to be willing to address—is not so much how we get people to read for transformation as opposed to information, but how do we get people to read the Bible at all. George Gallup Jr. is right: "Americans revere the Bible—but, by and large, they don't read it. And because they don't read it, they have become a nation of biblical illiterates."

The popular (and completely false) perception of the Bible is that it is a big, thick, black-covered book that is both unreadable and impossible to understand. Even long-time Christ-followers seem to have this opinion of God's best seller.

The greatest compliment

It's been my pleasure to author dozens of books. As an author, the greatest compliment you can pay me is to say, "I read your book." Please allow me to remind you that God wrote a book, and He only wrote one. What will you say to him in heaven, should He ask, "Did you read my book?" In your entire life, did you ever once read the only book God ever wrote?

The Bible is the unique revelation of God, and the promise of God is crystal clear:

"For as the rain and the snow come down from heaven and do not return there but water the earth, making it bring forth and sprout, giving seed to the sower and bread to the eater, so shall my word be that goes out from my mouth; it shall not return to me empty, but it shall accomplish that which I purpose, and shall succeed in the thing for which I sent it." Isaiah 55:10-11

God's Word will accomplish that which God purposes. That's good news indeed. How can we be transformed? How do we make progress on the road to spiritual maturity? Not through the mystical practices of the Desert Fathers or by stripping away the false self and discovering God at our center. Let the Buddhists believe that; you believe God's Word. The Bible is clearly God's sure-fire means to transform us and to change us from being infant believers into being strong and mature Christ-followers. The Bible is God's sure path. There is no other bottom line: the only provable, biblical key to spiritual formation is meaningful, consistent Bible engagement.

Begin anywhere, just begin

So, pick up your Bible, start reading wherever you'd like. When people ask me where they should begin reading the Bible I often ask, "If you went down to Barnes and Noble and bought a book, where would you start reading? Chapter 6? Chapter 22?" God's Word is a progressive revelation. Why not start where He started? At the beginning. But wherever you start—at Genesis or John—start!

Once you've read a portion of God's Word, take some time to reflect on it, meditate on it, let it marinate your heart and your mind. Let the Word of God dwell in you richly. Write down some things you learn for later reflection.

Then, respond to God's Word. Live out what you read, and start making some real progress toward spiritual maturity. Let the Bible change your life. Let God lead you to fulfillment and spiritual maturity by what He has already revealed to you in His Word. It's only difficult if you make it so.

Gentlemen (and Ladies), start your engines! It's time we got going. God has a sure path to spiritual maturity and to His heart. You can find it. Look for it in His Word—the Bible.

ABOUT THE AUTHOR

Woodrow Michael Kroll served for nearly 23 years as the President and Senior Bible Teacher of the international media ministry Back to the Bible. His *Back to the Bible* radio broadcasts, offered in multiple languages, were able to be heard by more than 50 percent of the world's population every day.

Dr. Kroll is the author of more than 50 books. He has earned M.A., M.Div., Th.M. and Doctor of Theology degrees and has done additional graduate study at Harvard, Princeton, the University of Virginia and the University of Strasbourg (France). Dr. Kroll is also known for his passion to increase Bible literacy by engaging people in the Bible and connecting them with the Author. Since 1980 he has waged war against creeping Bible illiteracy in the Church, speaking at many venues and writing multiple books on the subject. *Marginalized!* is another in a succession of these challenging books. "My greatest privilege," says Woodrow Kroll, "is preaching the Word of God."

His wife Linda and he reside in Ashland, Nebraska. They have four married children, sixteen grandchildren and one great grandchild.

APPENDIX A

The Center for Bible Engagement
Lincoln, Nebraska

History

The Center for Bible Engagement was founded on November 13, 2003 when Dr. Woodrow Kroll asked permission of the Board of Back to the Bible to launch a new division of its ministry called The Bible Literacy Center (BLC). This research and development corporation was founded to study the problem of Bible illiteracy in America and discover solutions to that problem. As founder, Dr. Kroll charged the research team to determine scientifically the answer to this question: "Why do so many people own Bibles and so few read them?" The BLC was dedicated to the memory of Clarence W. Hottel, Sr. who had a deep passion to see men and women everywhere engaged in a meaningful relationship with God. Mr. Hottel knew that kind of relationship could only happen when a person reads his or her Bible. The organization soon expanded beyond the research done by the BLC into The Center for Bible Engagement (CBE) which has become a major world center addressing both Bible illiteracy and Bible engagement. As the CBE continues to collect and analyze data, the results are shared with pastors, parents and other Christian leaders to allow them to influence the next generation to become fully engaged in God's Word. Products and programs are also introduced to allow people to have contact with God and His Word on multiple occasions throughout the day using social media.

CBE Leadership

Dr. Woodrow Kroll, Founder

As both President and Senior Bible Teacher for the international media ministry Back to the Bible, Dr. Woodrow Kroll already had his hands full. But he also had a passion to do more than "bless" his audience. For more than 30 years he had a deepening concern over the plague of Bible illiteracy infecting the Church and Christian community. That concern was given a voice and found a constructive outlet when he founded The Center for Bible Engagement. Today, he continues to be a principle spokesman for Bible engagement across America as well as a world-class teacher of God's Word around the world.

Dr. Arnie Cole, Director of Research & Development

With his passion for research and helping others, Dr. Arnie Cole has been active in developing methodologies, processes and best practices to instill significant behavioral change in individuals for most of his professional life. He received his BA & MA in Psychology, and the Doctor of Education degree in Institutional Management from Pepperdine University. Dr. Cole has been a pioneer in his field of research which led him to start three organizations in California that specialized in behavioral and social training for people with severe disabilities and violent behaviors

Dr. Pam Ovwigho, Research Director

A desire to turn data into information that answers important questions and solves vexing problems fuels Dr. Pam Ovwigho's professional life. With a B.A. in Psychology (Penn State University) and a Ph.D. in Human Services Psychology (University of Maryland), Pam has used her research, measurement, and analytic skills to tackle a wide variety of issues from family violence to spiritual growth. Serving as a research director at the University of Maryland for 15 years, Pam Ovwigho has authored dozens of academic journal articles and white papers. As the CBE's research director, Dr. Ovwigho conducts studies on Scripture engagement and spiritual growth.

Research Methods

Since 2005, The Center for Bible Engagement has surveyed more than 80,000 Americans and 10,000 people around the world about their spiritual lives. Some surveys focused on specific groups and were conducted in person – such as people who attend church regularly or youth attending a Christian event – while others drew from random samples of the general American population.

Survey Sampling International (SSI) conducts the studies based on random samples of the American population. SSI maintains 24 proprietary survey panels worldwide composed of a total of about 1.6 million people. SSI recruits people to its survey pools through 3400 different broadcast points on various Internet sites. To join the pool, respondents have to answer a series of screening questions and have their names and addresses validated against U.S. mail records. Once they are in the pool, respondents periodically receive invitations to participate in certain surveys. The incentive to complete a survey is entry into a drawing for a prize.

The CBE utilizes both open- and closed-ended questions in its studies. For example, they often ask participants an open-ended question like "How does God communicate with you?" Responses to this question are then coded using text analytic software (SPSS Text Analytics for Surveys®). The closed-ended questions include several scales that the CBE has developed. Two such scales measure what is termed "behavioral risks" and "relational risks." The original scale consists of 11 different behaviors but the CBE asks tweens to rate on a 6-point scale how often they participate in each behavior.

Factor analysis[75] revealed that the scale measures two different types of behaviors. One factor, which the CBE calls "Behavioral Risks," consists of smoking, drinking, sexual activity, viewing pornography, sexting, and gambling. Compared to other behaviors measured, these share the common characteristic that they are prohibited by society and, for tweens, are limited by parental monitoring and control. Four other behaviors — gossiping, cheating, lying, teasing or bullying others, and destructive thoughts – loaded on the second factor, "Relational Risks." Common traits for these behaviors are that they concern our relationships with others, are beyond the direct control of parents and may be more morally ambiguous. Cronbach's alpha reveals both scales have acceptable internal reliability.[76]

Whatever the type of question used, the CBE ensures that they are worded in ways that are clear, concise, and don't bias responses. In addition, they include items to test for response biases as well. For testing the hypotheses, the CBE uses bi-variate and multivariate statistical tests. Bi-variate analyses frequently include chi-square, t-tests, and correlations. Our multivariate models are typically multiple regression analyses and logit models.

As Zora Neal Hurston once commented, "Research is formalized curiosity. It is poking and prying with a purpose." Our purpose is to discover the truth about how respondents interact with God through His Word and develop programs and methods to make that interaction more meaningful, more consistent, and more life-changing.

APPENDIX B

CBE Significant Findings

Since its inception, The Center for Bible Engagement has been providing the Christian and non-Christian public with vital information about the impact the Bible has on the lives of individuals. If you are a visual learner, you will appreciate seeing some of those findings in graph form. For complete information and additional findings go to www.centerforbibleengagement.org or stop by and visit the Center at 6400 Cornhusker, Lincoln, Nebraska 68517. Here are some of the major findings from The Center for Bible Engagement that bear directly on spiritual formation and progress in growth toward spiritual maturity.

Springboards and Speed Bumps to Bible Reading

Anyone who has tried to read the Bible consistently knows it isn't easy. There are many speed bumps along the way that slow you down. In fact, they can inhibit your progress so much they actually discourage you and fuel that universal human tendency to give up when things get tough. But what are those speed bumps? What are the things that most people say keep them from reading their Bible? The Center for Bible Engagement asked 8,665 people from across the United States in a 113-question survey (November 2006) to answer that question honestly. Respondents to the survey were given space to write their own answers, as much or as little as they wanted. Since the survey excluded the general public, nearly all those who responded (99.7%) said they were followers of Jesus Christ with 75% saying they had been followers for more than ten years.

Consistent with other studies, a disconnect was discovered between respondents' expressed beliefs about the importance of the Bible and their reading habits. The vast majority of respondents indicated that the Bible is relevant to their everyday lives and is their life authority. However, only one-half read the Bible daily, with another 37% reading it more than once a week, but not daily. Only two out of five of these Christ-followers have read the entire Bible.

As noted earlier in this book, the number one reason people gave for being lax in reading God's Word is time. "I just don't have time," or "I'm too busy" were the most common answers to the survey. But in the graph below, you learn some of the other answers given in order of frequency.

Figure 1
What hinders you from reading the Bible regularly?

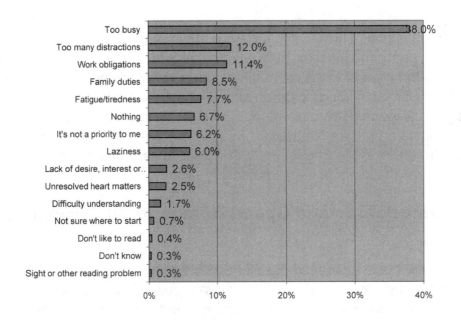

Notice the top five reason responses for not reading the Bible. While these are legitimate things, like work obligations and family duties, there is a ring of same-ness about all of them. They all look like subsets of excuse number seven—it's not a priority or number nine—lack of motivation. You know as well as I that we find time to do the things that are important to us, the things that truly matter to us. Work matters; you have to pay the bills. Family matters; they are God's gift to you. But if there isn't enough time left in your day to read God's Word, what does that say to God about how much He matters to you? I don't want to lay a guilt trip on you, but these are honest questions and deserve honest answers. If you have time to read the morning news, why don't you have time to read God's Word? If you have time to read all your emails (even junk emails), why don't you have time to read the Bible? If you have time to mutter something on Facebook, why don't you have time to muse over what you've read in the only Book God ever wrote? Is the gut answer simply that it isn't a priority with you? Think about it, and give yourself an honest answer.

My observation is that the first five excuses relate to the daily pressures of life, the same pressures that Jesus pointed out in the parable of the sower choke the Word and cause it to be unfruitful, i.e. the cares of the world, the deceitfulness of riches and the desires for other things (Mark 4:13-20). The second tier of five excuses appear to address laziness or a lack of motivation as hindering factors to engaging God's Word. We have to track all the way to excuse number 11 and the bottom tier of excuses before we encounter expressions like "Difficulty understanding" or "Not sure where to start." Honest people gave honest answers and the honest truth is that you cannot blame the Bible for a lack of Bible engagement. The bottom tier of excuses accounts for just 2.7% of total while the top tier accounts for a whopping 77.6% of total.

Conversely, the CBE asked the same respondents what helped them read their Bibles. What were the springboards to consistent Bible reading? Again, people were given opportunity to write their own answers not pick from a few suggested answers. I think some answers will surprise you.

Figure 2
What helps you read the Bible regularly?

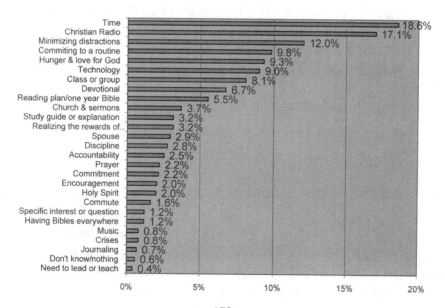

Speed bumps and spring boards. But you don't need to be a scholar, a researcher or a statistician to see some very telling things in these responses. For example, notice that time is the lead answer for why people don't read the Bible as well as for why they do. Although we all have exactly the same amount of time in a day, some people have more disposable time than others. And look at what finding the right fit for you in a Bible reading aid meant in keeping you going (Christian radio, a spouse, prayer, a routine, etc.). Similarly, see how adopting the right attitude played a role toward engaging God's Word (discipline, account-ability, commitment, etc.).

It's significant that when people were given an opportunity to respond anonymously they give honest, forthright answers, answers right from the heart. The real problem in failing to read the Bible is not time or relevance or difficulty; the real problem is that it just isn't a priority with us. We lack the "want to." We have marginalized God and His Word in our lives and we are only beginning to recognize how much that has cost us.

Communication with God

One of the key issues in spiritual formation, as pointed out in chapter one of this book, is how we communicate with God and how He communicates with us. Christianity is unique among religions in its emphasis on a relationship between God and man and for that relationship to grow and mature, it must include regular two-way communication whereby the follower of Christ both hears from God and talks with Him.

The CBE has been most interested in how those in the first half of their lives communicate with God so three separate surveys were done with three different age demographics seeking that information. Even more specifically, these surveys were done among Christian populations, those who indicate they are born-again Christians.

Children ages 8 through 12

The data in the next five paragraphs comes from an Internet-based survey with a random sample of 1,009 American children between the ages of 8 and 12. The 45-item survey instrument used in this study contains a mix of closed- and open-ended questions about children's involvement in attending religious services, prayer, Bible reading on their own and with their family, their beliefs about how God communicates with them and how they communicate with God. In order to understand better how children perceive communication with God, two simple open-ended questions were included, the first: "How do you communicate with God?" followed by: "How does God communicate with you?" Answers to these questions were analyzed using SPSS Text Analysis.

The majority of children (75.9%) indicate they communicate with God through prayer. Most often their open-ended answers were "by praying" or "through prayer." Fewer than one in ten (7.8%) stated either they do not communicate with God or they do not believe in God. Prayer was the near universal method of talking *with* God.

There was greater diversity, however, in answer to the second question about *how God talks with them.* More than one in ten (13.7%) said they did not know how God communicates with them and an additional 8.4% felt that God does not communicate with them at all. The Bible or God's Word was mentioned by 11.5% of children. Their answers to this open-ended question were often "when I read the Bible I find the answer" or "not sure, but when I read the Bible something inside tells me stuff." However, many answers showed either a lack of understanding of God's method of communication or that the Bible was not alone in God's communications options. Here are other open-ended answers. "Through the good things that happen to me." "Helping me be a good person." "I just feel better on the inside like He is with me." "Sunshine and beautiful things." "He shows himself to me in nature and friends."

While 54.5% of the child respondents to this survey identified themselves as Christian/Protestant and 15.3% identified themselves as Roman Catholic, clearly they did not have an intuitive understanding that God speaks to them through His Word.

Early teens ages 13 through 17

A random sample of 808 youth between the ages of 13 and 17 (with respondents averaging 15 years old at the time and two-thirds of them [66.6%] in high school) revealed similar findings. Again, 41.8% of respondents identified themselves as Christian/Protestant and 20.2% identified themselves as Roman Catholic. When teens were asked to describe how they communicate with God, by far the most common answer given by two out of three teens was through prayer. Most simply used the word "pray" or "prayer" while others elaborated more fully. "I talk to him all the time. He is everywhere, in my mind I speak to him." "I pray when I go to bed at night." "I just talk like He is there with me." After prayer, the next most common response was that the teen did not communicate at all with God. A little more than one-tenth of teens gave an answer along these lines, some simply saying, "I don't" while others expressed the belief that God does not exist so they could not communicate with Him.

To the question "How do you feel God communicates with you?" even more varied responses were given. Figure 3 shows the responses to how God talks to teens.

Figure 3
How teens feel God communicates with them

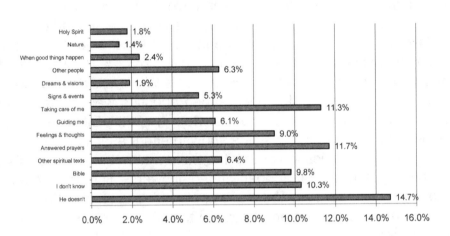

Sadly, few teens – about one in ten (9.8%) – listed the Bible as God's method of communicating with them. Children and young teens, even those who attend church and grow up in Christian homes, are not making the connection between the Bible and God speaking to them. In fact, the most common theme in answering the question about how God communicates with them was that He does not communicate at all. This was the answer given by 14.7% of respondents. An additional one-tenth said they didn't know. Most answers simply stated "He doesn't" or "I don't know." Others said, "He has not yet personally communicated with me" or "so far I haven't seen it." It is evident that these teens either believe God is silent or if He should choose to communicate with them it will be as He did with Moses or with Paul on the road to Damascus. The Bible just didn't enter the minds of the majority of teens when asked about God's communication methods. Little wonder people are seeking spirituality in all the wrong places if the right place cannot be identified by them.

Is there any discernible connection between engaging God's Word consistently and meaningfully and believing that God communicates with these teens? Indeed there is. Table 1 crosses the Bible reading habits of teens with their understanding of how God speaks to them. Consistent with similar findings among adults, the teens who are more engaged in God's Word (4 or more times each week) are more likely to say that God communicates with them through the Bible and far less likely to say God doesn't communicate with them or they don't know how He communicates. The connection between reading God's Word consistently and hearing from God through His Word is firmly established.

Table 1
Bible engagement and communication with God

How God Communicates with You	Bible Reading			
	0 days	1-3 days	4 or more days	
Feelings & thoughts	4.8%	12.5%	11.2%	**
Guides me on how to act	3.2%	8.6%	7.7%	**
Bible	2.3%	12.9%	22.4%	***
Answered prayers	7.2%	12.5%	18.2%	**
Takes care of me	10.4%	12.5%	6.3%	
Other people	2.8%	8.6%	9.8%	**
Holy Spirit	0.7%	1.7%	4.2%	*
He doesn't	22.4%	4.3%	0.7%	***
Don't know	13.9%	5.6%	2.1%	***

*p < .05, **p < .01, ***p < .001

(Center for Bible Engagement. 2006. *Bible literacy and spiritual growth: Survey*)

Mosaics

Researcher George Barna coined the term "Mosaic Generation" to refer to those born between 1984 and 2002. This age demographic is also known as Generation Y or Millennials. In terms of spirituality, Mosaics tend to be moral pragmatists, deciding questions of morality based on "whatever works." Mosaics are typified by the belief that there is no absolute truth and whatever is right for you is right, but it may not be right for them.

Through an Internet-based survey with a random sample of 987 Americans between the ages of 18 and 24, a 45-item survey instrument contained a mix of closed- and open-ended questions about involvement in attending religious services, prayer, the Bible, how God communicates with you and how you communicate with Him. Of this group, 28.2% identified themselves as Christian/Protestant and 16.1% as Roman Catholic. Characteristic of this university-age group, 19.3% of respondents identified themselves as having no religious affiliation, 17.9% said they were "spiritual," 7% were atheist and 3.1% were agnostic.

To the question of how Mosaics communicate with God, three-fifths (61.8%) say they talk with God through prayer (which is consistently the number one answer of every age group). However, the next most common response, given by 29.9%, is that they do not communicate with God at all or they do not believe in God.

When asked how Mosaics believed God communicates with them, one out of four young adults said that He does not communicate with them. An additional one-tenth indicated that they did not know how God communicates with them. Only 7.6% mentioned the Bible. Some mentioned God's Word specifically while others included the Bible in a list of several ways that God uses to communicate. This parallels the marginalization of the Bible seen in much of the discussion of spiritual formation today where the Bible is lumped in with other spiritual disciplines as the way to become intimate with God.

One reason Mosaics have difficulty understanding that God speaks to them through His Word is that typically Mosaics are not huge Bible engagers. Even those who identified themselves as born-again were less likely ever to read the Bible than they were to read it four or more times a week, the amount necessary for life change, shedding destructive habits and replacing them with habits that lead to growth toward spiritual maturity. See Figure 4.

Figure 4
Days reading or listening to the Bible in the past week

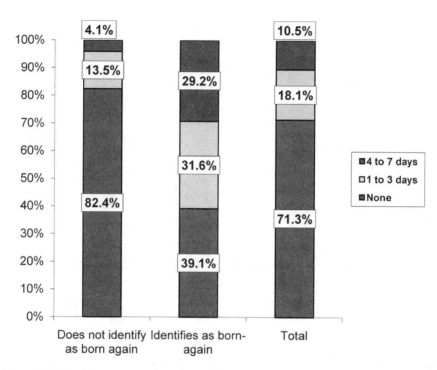

Center for Bible Engagement. (2009). *Bible engagement, communication with God, and the Mosaic generation.* Lincoln, NE: Center for Bible Engagement. Available online: http://www.centerforbibleengagement.org/index.php?option=com_content&task=view&id=33&Itemid

Bible Illiteracy and Spiritual Growth

Just as smoking has been one of the chief causes of lung cancer, Bible illiteracy (not the lack of ability to read the Bible but the lack of desire to read it) has been one of the chief causes of stunted spiritual growth. You simply cannot grow to the full measure of Jesus Christ if you aren't in the Word daily and growing in grace and the knowledge of our Lord and Savior Jesus Christ (2 Peter 3:18).

In order to chart Bible literacy, several years ago I developed a scale where people could make a personal determination of their relationship to God's Word.

Figure 5
The Kroll Bible Literacy Scale

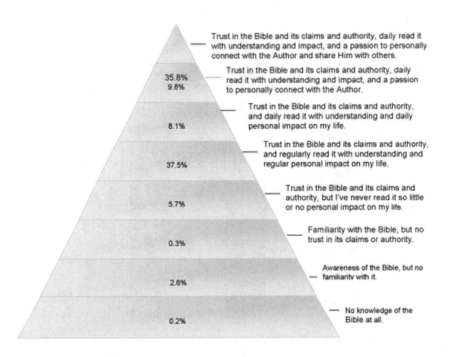

The Kroll Bible Literacy Scale features eight levels of awareness and trust in the Bible ranging from no knowledge at all (and therefore no trust) to total trust in the Bible and a passion to connect with its Author and share Him with others. Everyone finds himself or herself somewhere on this scale, from the most remote sinner to the most revered saint. See where do you think you are?

The Center for Bible Engagement used the Kroll Bible Literacy Scale to ask respondents to rate themselves with regard to their trust in the Bible. Among the survey sample, a little more than one third (35.8%) chose the highest level. The next most common response, indicated by 37.5% of participants, is the fifth level of the scale: "Trust in the Bible and its claims and authority and regularly read it with understanding and regular personal impact on my life." The Kroll Scale also helped to determine the synergistic relationship between Bible reading frequency, Bible memorization and knowledge of the contents of the Bible. The more frequently a person read the Bible with the more time spent each day in the Word and time spent memorizing verses, the more respondents knew about the Bible and the more likely they were to read the Bible all the way through. For each additional Bible verse respondents had memorized in the past year, the probability of reading the Bible daily compared to not at all increased by 69.7%. Among those who have read the Bible completely, 65.4% indicated that they read the Bible daily. In contrast, only one-third (34.0%) of respondents who have not read the Bible completely reported daily reading.

Figure 6
The relationship between Bible reading frequency and knowledge

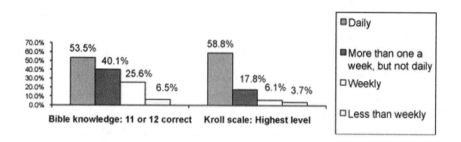

There can be no doubt that consistent, meaningful Bible engagement is the first step toward Bible understanding just as Bible understanding is the first step toward an intimate knowledge with God and growth toward spiritual maturity. As noted in this book, Bible reading for content alone is not the transformation we need for spiritual maturity; it is but the first step. But those who marginalize the Bible and diminish the importance of this first step are never able to take the second step and the third step on the quest for spiritual maturity.

As I have consistently maintained throughout this book, the reason so little Bible engagement takes place in the lives of Christ-followers when they claim the Bible is so important to them is not a lack of Bibles, a lack of time or even a lack of desire. But there is a disconnect between desire and priority. People want to grow spiritually but they simply don't make it a priority.

Defining Spiritual Maturity

One final area of scientific investigation with regard to the subject of this book is what survey respondents believe about growth toward spiritual maturity. Spiritual formation is on the minds of just about everyone today. Take a look at your church's mission statement. Likely there will be some statement about helping members grow to spiritual maturity. Go to any church website and may well find the same. No church wishing to honor the lordship of Christ can ignore the third third of His

Great commission – "teaching them to observe all that I have commanded you" (Matthew 28:20). That is task one in the local church's role of "warning everyone and teaching everyone with all wisdom, that we may present everyone mature in Christ" (Colossians 1:28). But articulating this as part of the mission of the local church and getting members to experience growth toward spiritual maturity, or even to identify what spiritual maturity is, are two drastically different things.

Is it possible that the quest for spiritual maturity is made even more difficult because those pursuing it can't even define what spiritual maturity is? Can anyone achieve spiritual maturity without a clear understanding of what they're searching for? Likely not, but identifying what spiritual maturity actually is seems to be a problem for many Christ-followers. A 2009 Barna survey concluded that an underlying reason why there is little progress in helping people develop spiritually is that many churchgoers and clergy struggle to articulate a basic understanding of spiritual maturity. "People aspire to be spiritually mature, but they do not know what it means. Pastors want to guide others on the path to spiritual wholeness, but they are often not clearly defining the goals or the outcomes of that process." (The Barna Group, "Many Churchgoers and Faith Leaders Struggle to Define Spiritual Maturity," May 11, 2009). Researchers at The Center for Bible Engagement discovered the same struggles. The Center concluded: "Given a lack of consensus on the terms among the Christian community, it's not surprising to find considerable diversity among the definitions given by teens and adults from various faith backgrounds." As shown in Figure 7, more than one-fifth of responses provided only a vague definition of spiritual maturity, such as: to know what you do or say; you grow with God; to be mature in thoughts words and deeds; or experience with God.

Figure 7
Definitions of Spiritual Maturity

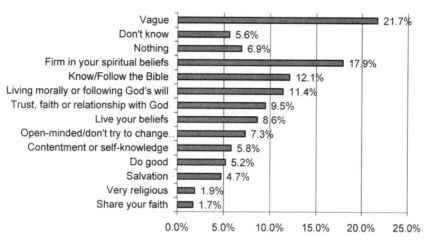

Center for Bible Engagement. (2010). *Americans' views of spiritual growth and maturity.* Lincoln, NE: Author. Available online: http://www.centerforbibleengagement.org/index. php?option=com_content&task=view&id=33&Itemid

It is remarkable that many of the themes evident in Americans' definitions of spiritual maturity reflect only the very beginning stages of what Christians view as spiritual growth. For example, some responses defined spiritual maturity as having a relationship with God (9.5%) or having accepted Jesus Christ as your personal Savior (4.7%). But this is not spiritual maturity; this is salvation, only the first step on the road to spiritual maturity. If we can't distinguish between salvation and service, if we can't define the journey and understand the end goals of spiritual growth, how can we ever expect to achieve them?

David Kinnaman, President of the Barna Group, sums up: "America has a spiritual depth problem partly because the faith community does not have a robust definition of its spiritual goals." Research at The Center for Bible Engagement confirms this.

BIBLIOGRAPHY

Inclusion in this bibliography does not constitute an endorsement of any book. Rather, the bibliography is designed to present a broad spectrum of books on the subjects of spiritual formation, spiritual maturity and Bible engagement.

Keith R. Anderson, and Randy D. Reese, *Spiritual Mentoring: A Guide for Seeking and Giving Direction* (Downers Grove, IL, InterVarsity Press, 1999).

R. H. Barton, *Invitation to Solitude and Silence: Experiencing God's Transforming Presence* (Downers Grove, IL, InterVarsity Press, 2004).

_____ *Sacred Rhythms: Arranging Our Lives for Spiritual Transformation* (Downers Grove, InterVarsity Press, 2006).

Donald Bloesch, *Faith and Its Counterfeits* (Downers Grove, IL: InterVarsity, 1981).

_____, The Crisis of Piety (Colorado Springs: Helmers & Howard, 1988).

Kenneth Boa, *Conformed to His Image: Biblical and Practical Approaches to Spiritual Formation* (Grand Rapids, MI, Zondervan, 2001).

Dietrich Bonhoeffer, *The Cost of Discipleship* (New York, Touchstone, 1959).

W. R. Bright, Ed. *Teacher's Manual for Ten Basic Steps Toward Christian Maturity* (San Bernardino, CA, Campus Crusade for Christ, International, 1965).

_____, A Handbook for Christian Maturity (New*Life* Publications, 1994).

Lewis Sperry Chafer, He That is Spiritual (Grand Rapids, MI: Zondervan, 1983).

Henry Cloud and John Townsend, How People Grow: What the Bible Reveals About Personal Growth (Grand Rapids, MI: Zondervan, 2004).

The Cloud of Unknowing (New York, NY: HarperOne, 2004).

Elmer Dyck, ed. The Act of Bible Reading (Downers Grove, IL: Inter Varsity Press, 1996).

Gordon D. Fee and Douglas Stuart, How to Read the Bible for All It's Worth (Grand Rapids, MI: Zondervan, 1981).

_____, How to Read the Bible Book by Book, (Grand Rapids, MI: Zondervan, 202).

Richard J. Foster, *Celebration of Discipline: The Path To Spiritual Growth* (London, Hodder & Stoughton, 1989).

_____, *Prayer: Finding the Heart's True Home* (San Francisco: HarperSanFrancisco, 1992).

J. Fowler, Stages of Faith: *The Psychology of Human Development and the Quest for Meaning* (San Francisco: Harper & Row, 1981)

Kenneth O. Gangel and James C. Wilhoit, The Christian Educator's Handbook on Spiritual Formation (Grand Rapids, MI: Baker Books, 1998).

L. L. Graybeal and J. L. Roller, Living the Mission: A Spiritual Formation Guide (New York, HarperOne, 2007).

Jeffrey P. Greenman, ed. and George Kalantzis, ed. Life in the Spirit: Spiritual Formation in Theological Perspective. (Downers Grove, IL: InterVarsity Press, 2010).

Douglas Groothuis, Truth Decay Defending Christianity Against the Challenges of Postmodernism (Downers Grove, IL: IVP Books, 2000).

F. J. Huegel, Bone of His Bone (Maitland, FL: Christian Books Publishing House, 1997).

M. Ivens, *Understanding the Spiritual Exercises* (Leominster, Gracewing, 1998).

Arthur L. Johnson, Faith Misguided Exposing the Dangers of Mysticism (Chicago: Moody, 1988).

Woodrow Kroll, Taking Back the Good Book: How America Forgot the Bible and Why It Matters to You (Wheaton, IL: Crossway, 2007)

Tim LaHaye, How to Study the Bible for Yourself (Eugene, OR: Harvest House, 2006).

Brother Lawrence *The Practice of the Presence of God* (New Kensington, PA, Whitaker House, 1982).

Mel Lawrenz, The Dynamics of Spiritual Formation (Grand Rapids: Baker, 2000).

Richard Lovelace, *Dynamics of Spiritual Life* (Downers Grove, IL: InterVarsity, 1979).

John MacArthur, *Keys to Spiritual Growth* (Old Tappan, NJ: Revell, 1978).

_____, How to Study the Bible (Chicago: Moody, 2009).

_____, The Keys to Spiritual Growth (Wheaton, IL: Crossway, 2001).

Richard Mayhue, Spiritual Maturity (Wheaton, IL: Victor Books, 1992).

B. McGinn, *The Mystical Thought of Meister Eckhart: The Man from Whom God Hid Nothing* (New York: The Crossroad Publishing Company, 2001).

Alistair McGrath, *Beyond the Quiet Time: Practical Evangelical Spirituality* (Grand Rapids, MI, Baker Books, 1995).

Thomas Merton, Contemplative Prayer (Colorado Springs, CO: Image; 1971).

_____, Spiritual Direction and Meditation (Collegeville, MN: Liturgical Press 1960)

Thomas Merton and Dalai Lama XIV, The Way of Chuang Tzu (New York, NY: New Directions, 2010).

Robert Mulholland, *Invitation to a Journey: A Road Map for Spiritual Formation* (Downers Grove, IL: InterVarsity, 1993).

_____, *Shaped by the Word: The Power of Scripture in Spiritual Formation* (Nashville: Upper Room, 1986).

Andrew Murray, *Like Christ: Thoughts on the Blessed Life of Conformity to the Son of God* (London: James Nisbet, 1896).

Gary C. Newton, Growing Toward Spiritual Maturity (Wheaton, IL: Crossway, 2004).

M. B. Pennington, *Centering Prayer: Renewing an Ancient Christian Prayer Form* (New York, Doubleday, 1980).

_____, *True Self, False Self: Unmasking the Spirit Within* (New York, The Crossroad Publishing Company, 2000).

Eugene H. Peterson, *Christ Plays in Ten Thousand Places: A Conversation in Spiritual Theology* (Grand Rapids, MI., William B. Eerdmans Publishing Company, 2005).

_____, *Eat This Book: A Conversation in the Art of Spiritual Reading* (Grand Rapids, MI, William B. Eerdmans Publishing Company, 2006).

_____, *Subversive Spirituality* (Grand Rapids, MI., William B. Eerdmans Publishing Company, 1997).

Stephen Prothero, Bible Literacy: What Every American Needs to Know—but Doesn't (New York, NY: Harper Collins, 2007).

H. L. Rice, Reformed Spirituality: An Introduction for Believers (Louisville, Westminster/John Knox Press, 1991).

Oswald Sanders, Spiritual Maturity: Principles of Spiritual Growth For every Believer (Chicago: Moody, 1994).

Francis Schaeffer, *True Spirituality* (Wheaton, IL: Tyndale, 1972)

P. Sheldrake, Ed. *The New Westminster Dictionary of Christian Spirituality* (Louisville, KN, John Knox Press, 2005).

J. B. Smith, *A Spiritual Formation Workbook: Small Group Resources for Nurturing Christian Growth* (New York, HarperCollins Publisher, 1991).

R. C. Sproul, *Knowing Scripture* (Downers Grove, IL: InterVarsity, 1977).

George Sweeting, How to Continue the Christian Life (Chicago: Moody, 1998).

G. Thomas, *Sacred Pathways* (Grand Rapids, MI, Zondervan Publishing House, 1996).

Elmer Towns, A *Beginner's Guide to Reading the Bible*.

A. W. Tozer, *Tozer on the Holy Spirit, a 366-Day Devotional*, Compiled by Marilynne E. Foster. Camp Hill, PA: Christian Publications, Inc. p. December 21.

Brad Waggoner, *The Shape of Faith to Come: Spiritual Formation and the Future of Discipleship*. (LifeWay).

Robert Webber, *Ancient-Future Time: Forming Spirituality through the Christian Year* (Grand Rapids, MI, Baker Books, 2004).

_____, *The Divine Embrace: Recovering the Passionate Spiritual Life* (Grand Rapids, MI, Baker Books, 2006).

Donald S. Whitney, Spiritual Disciplines for the Christian Life (Colorado Springs, CO: NavPress, 1997).

James C. Wilhoit, *Spiritual Formation as if the Church Mattered: Growing in Christ through Community* (Grand Rapids, MI, Baker Academic, 2008).

Dallas Willard, *Renovation of the Heart: Putting on the Character of Christ* (Colorado Springs, CO., NavPress, 2002).

_____, *The Spirit of the Disciplines: Understanding How God Changes Lives* (New York, HarperCollins Publisher, 1991).

Dallas Willard and D. Simpson, Revolution *of Character: Discovering Christ's Pattern for Spiritual Transformation* (Colorado Springs, CO, NavPress, 2005).

Ray Yungen, A Time of Departing (Eureka, MT: Lighthouse Trails Publishing, 2006).

ENDNOTES

1 A. W. Tozer, *Tozer on the Holy Spirit, a 366-Day Devotional*, Compiled by Marilynne E. Foster. Camp Hill, PA: Christian Publications, Inc. p. January 26.

2 Matthew 22:44; Mark 12:36; Luke 20:42; Acts 2:34

3 There are many more instances, e.g. Nahum 1:1, Habakkuk 1:1, Zephaniah 1:1, Haggai 1:1-2, Zechariah 1:1 and Malachi 1:1.

4 A. W. Tozer, *Tozer on the Holy Spirit, a 366-Day Devotional*, Compiled by Marilynne E. Foster. Camp Hill, PA: Christian Publications, Inc. p. December 21.

5 See Mark 7:8

6 Arthur L. Johnson, *Faith Misguided: Exposing the Dangers of Mysticism.* Chicago: Moody, 1988, p. 91.

7 Arnold Cole and Pamela Caudill Ovwigho, Bible Engagement & Social Behavior: How Familiarity & Frequency of Contact with the Bible Affects One's Behavior, 2009. See the full study at: http://www.centerforbibleengagement.org/images/stories/pdfScientific_Evidence_for_the_Power_of_4.pdfaccessedJanuary2010.

8 The Center for Bible Engagement: Mature Believers' Understanding of Spiritual Growth. Results from the 2009 Radio Listener Study, November 2009.

9 William Hendrickson, *The Gospel of John*. Grand Rapids: Baker, 1981. p. 52.

10 R. A. Torrey, *Person and Work of the Holy Spirit*, rev. ed. Grand Rapids: Zondervan, 1974, p. 123.

11 Nouthetic Counseling is a form of Christian counseling developed by Jay E. Adams in the late 1960s and published in his 1970 book, *Competent to Counsel*. Adams named his approach after the New Testament Greek word *noutheteō* variously translated as "admonish", "correct" or "exhort." Adams himself emphasized the meaning "confront" in the development of his counseling methods.

12 C.S. Lewis, The Silver Chair (New York: Harper Collins, 1953), 27.

13 From "Sometimes Fairy Stories May Say Best What's to Be Said," in Of Other Words, ed. Walter Hooper (New York: Harcourt Brace Jovanovich, 1966).

[14] C.S. Lewis, "Letter to Ruth Broady," dated October 26, 1963, in *Letters to Children*, ed. Lyle Dorsett (New York: Macmillan, 1985), 111.

[15] C.S. Lewis, *They Stand Together: The Letters of C.S. Lewis to Arthur Greeves* (New York: Macmillan, 1979), 135.

[16] C.S. Lewis, *Mere Christianity,* (San Francisco: Harper San Francisco, © 1952, C.S. Lewis Pte. Ltd.), 164.

[17] Note: Much more has been written on C.S. Lewis's writing and his conversion to Christianity. Take a look at: *The Most Reluctant Convert* by David C. Dowing; *C.S. Lewis: Lightbearer in the Shadowlands* by Angus J.L. Menuge; and *C.S. Lewis* by Ruth James Cording.

[18] Related to this subject, there is an excellent Internet article entitled "The Marks of Manhood" by Dr. Albert Mohler, president of the Southern Baptist Theological Seminary in Louisville, Kentucky. Dr. Mohler lists thirteen "sufficiencies" necessary to exhibit maturity in various areas of life. You can find the article at: http://www.boundless.org/2005/articles/a0001093.cfm

[19] John Calvin's Bible Commentary, http://www.sacred-texts.com/chr/calvin/cc38/cc38015.htm.

[20] C. E. B. Cranfield, *The Epistle to the Romans: Romans 9-16: A Critical and Exegetical Commentary.* Edinburgh: T & T Clarke Publishers, 1979, p. 600.

[21] Walter Bauer's *A Greek-English Lexicon of the New Testament* (based on *Griechish-Deutsches Worterbuch)*. Chicago: University Of Chicago Press; 3rd edition, 2001.

[22] Henry George Liddell, Robert Scott and James Morris Whilton, *A Lexicon Abridged from Liddell and Scott's Greek-English Lexicon.* Charleston, S.C.: Nabu Press, 2010.

[23] From the Center for the Study of Global Christianity at Gordon-Conwell Theological Seminary, 2009.

[24] http://www.gideons.org/AboutUs/WorldwideImact.aspx.

[25] C. S. Lewis, *Mere Christianity.* New York: The Macmillan Company, 1943, 1971, p. 123.

[26] J. I. Packer, forward to R. C. Sproul, *Knowing Scripture.* Downers Grove, IL: InterVarsity Press, 1979, pp. 9-10.

[27] G. S. Banhatti, *Life and Philosophy of Swami Vivekananda.* Atlantic Publishers & Distributors, 1995. pp.43-44.

[28] Jeffrey Po, "Is Buddhism a Pessimistic Way of Life?" http://www.4ui.com/eart/172eart1.thm.

[29] Kosho Uchiyama, *Opening the Hand of Thought: Approach to Zen*, Penguin Books, New York, 1993, p. 98.

[30] The National Consultants for Education, Inc. http://www.nceducation.org/spiritual.html.

[31] W. T. Trace, *Mysticism and Philosophy*. New York: Palgrave Macmillan, 1960, p 79.

[32] Quoted in Otto Friedrich, "New Age harmonies, a strange mix of spirituality and superstition is sweeping across the country." Time. 130.n23 (Dec 7, 1987): 62(7).

[33] Robert Wuthnow, *After Heaven: Spirituality in America Since the 1950s*. Berkeley, CA: University of California Press, 1998, p. 4.

[34] http://blog.beliefnet.com/intenchopra/2009/01/obama-and-the-rise-of-secular.thml

[35] "Many Americans Mix Multiple Faiths" (December 9, 2009). The Pew Forum survey was conducted Aug. 11-27, 2009 see: http://www.pewforum.org/Other-Beliefs-and-Practices/Many-Americans-Mix-Multiple-Faiths.aspx.

[36] August 30th, 2008 by iMonk.

[37] Brad Waggoner, *The Shape of Faith to Come: Spiritual Formation and the Future of Discipleship,* Nashville, B&H Publishing.

[38] The Barna Update, September 27, 2005, "New Survey Shows Areas of Spiritual Life People Feel Most Confident About – and Those They Want Help With the Most."

[39] Donald S. Whitney, *Spiritual Disciplines for the Christian Life*. Colorado Springs, CO: NavPress, 1991. p. 15.

[40] Richard J. Foster, *Celebration of Discipline. The Path to Spiritual Growth*. New York: Harper & Row, Publishers, 1978.

[41] Dallas Willard, *The Spirit of the Disciplines. Understanding How God Changes Lives*. San Francisco: Harper San Francisco, 1988.

[42] http://www.prayingchurch.org/contemplative.html.

[43] Thomas Merton, *The Seven Story Mountain*. New York: Harcourt Brace & Company, 1999, p. 203.

[44] http://www.contemplativeoutreach.org/site/DocServer/MethodCP2008.pdf?docID=121.

[45] Thomas Keating, *Open Mind, Open Heart*. Amity, N.Y: Amity House, 1986, p. 97.

[46] Thomas Keating, *Finding Grace at the Center*. Manchester, UK: St. Bede's Publications, 1978, p. 20.

[47] Thomas Keating, *Intimacy With God*. New York: Crossroads Publishing Company, 2009. pp. 11-12.

[48] http://www.catholicculture.org/culture/library/view.cfm?id=6337&CFID=9731334&CFTOKEN=20677144

[49] Johnnette Benkovic, The New Age Counterfeit. Santa Barbara, CA: Queenship Publications, 2009.

[50] Finbarr Flanagan, "Centering Prayer: Transcendental Meditation for the Christian Market: "Faith and Renewal," May/June, 1991, p. 2.

[51] See Homilia Abulae habita in honorem Sanctae Teresiae: AAS 75 (1983), pp. 256-257.

[52] http://www.ewtn.com/library/curia/cdfmed.htm.

[53] http://www.contemplativeourtreach.org/site/News2?page=NewsArticle&id=5252.

[54] Thomas Keating, *Open Mind, Open Heart*. Amity, NY: Amity House, 1986, p.15.

[55] Thomas Keating, *Invitation to Love: The Way of Christian Contemplation*. New York: Continuum, 1994, p. 129.

[56] http://www.lcms.org/pages/internal.asp?NavID=6641.

[57] Tim Unsworth, "The ancient labyrinth makes a comeback: walk through maze recalls our wandering journey through life," National Catholic Reporter, October 3, 2003, (http://findarticles.com/p/articles/mi_m1141/is_42_39/ai_108838277/)

[58] Penelope Reed Doob, *The Idea of the Labyrinth from Classical Antiquity through the Middle Ages.* Ithaca, NY: Cornell University Press, 1992, p 36.

[59] Leadership Journal, Vol. 22, Issue 4, Fall 2001, http://www.christianitytoday.com/le/2001/fall/4.38.html.

[60] Ibid.

[61] http://www.lcms.org/pages/internal.asp?NavID=6641.

[62] Rev. Jill Geoffrion, Dedication of Deep Haven Labyrinth, http://jillkhg.com/labreded.html.

[63] The Labyrinth Society, http://www.labyrinthsociety.org.

[64] http://www.fisheaters.com/lectiodivina.html.

[65] http://www.fisheaters.com/lectiodivina.html.

[66] BusinessWeek, July 18, 2005, and Reuters, on *Harry Potter.* (13 July 2009).

[67] Russell Ash, Top 10 of Everything 2002. London: Dorling Kindersley, 2001.

[68] The Barna Update, "Christians Say They Do Best At Relationships, Worst In Bible Knowledge," June 14, 2005.

[69] Ibid.

[70] The Princeton Religion Research Center's study entitled "The Bible and the American People", Princeton, NJ, 2001, p. 6.

[71] Barna Research Online, "Discipleship Insights Revealed in New Book by George Barna," www.barna.org/cgi-bin/PagePressRelease.asp?=ID 76&Reference=E&Key=bible%20knowledgeNovember 28,2000.

[72] David F. Wells, *No Place for Truth or Whatever Happened to Evangelical Theology?* Grand Rapids: Eerdmans, 1993, p. 4.

[73] Postcard from San Diego: Fighting 'Bibliolatry' at the Evangelical Theological Society by Ted Olsen. Christianity Today, November 14, 2007.

[74] A.W. Tozer, When He Is Come" published Christian Publications, Inc. © 1968. The book is recommended and is now published under the title "The Counselor." http://www.twtministries.com/articles/tozer1.1.shtml.

[75] Factor analysis is a statistical procedure that uncovers relationships among many variables. It identifies the common dimensions or factors to which the variables can be reduced.

[76] For more information about these scales, please see Ovwigho, P.C. & Cole, A.R. (2010). Scriptural engagement, communication with God, and moral behavior among children. *International Journal of Children's Spirituality, 15*: 101-113.

INDEX

Lectio Divina   116, 132, 137, 138, 139, 140, 141.
Lewis, C. S.   54, 55, 56, 98.
Lowelle, Kimberly   137.
Luther, Martin   141.

Marechal, Paul   129.
Marginalize(d)   vii, ix, x, 20, 22, 30, 34, 35, 39, 44, 94, 146, 147, 165, 174, 181.
Meditation   ix, 17, 34, 35, 98, 99, 101, 106, 118, 125, 126, 127, 140, 145.
Memorizing Scripture   31, 98, 100, 101, 180.
Metabolize, Metabolization   34, 36, 39, 41, 43, 70, 74, 75, 98, 99, 101.
Mind of God   12, 13, 16, 17, 18, 19, 27, 38, 42, 74, 75, 90, 91, 96, 101, 152, 154, 158, 159.
Monasticism   23, 34, 41, 43, 48, 75, 94, 108, 111, 114, 122, 138, 139.
Monk(s) x. 30, 44, 52, 87, 101, 105, 108, 125, 126, 128, 129, 131, 139.
Moody, D. L.   59.
Mother Earth   ix, 107.
Moses   15, 33, 81, 82, 95, 96, 98, 99, 128, 154, 176.
Mystical   ix, 22, 75, 89, 94, 104, 106, 107, 108, 118, 119, 122, 125, 129, 130, 149, 157, 162.
Mystic, Mysticism   ix, x, 20, 22, 23, 30, 34, 37, 41, 44, 48, 52, 61, 63, 75, 87, 89, 94, 104, 105, 106, 107, 108, 109, 113, 115, 118, 119, 122, 125, 126, 127, 129, 130, 149, 157, 161, 162.

Native American Spirituality   107.
New Age   48, 107, 109, 129.
New Christian Spirituality, The   ix, 44, 94, 116, 123, 161.
New Testament   vii, 13, 15, 16, 33, 49, 55, 58, 66, 74 77, 82, 84, 85, 90, 92, 96, 97, 99, 120, 157, 158.

Obama, Barack   110.
Old Testament   vii, 13, 15, 16, 18, 49, 82, 98, 157 158.
Olsen, Ted   146.

Packer, J. I.   102
Pastor(s) vii, ix, 22, 23, 27, 48, 56, 57, 58, 69, 70, 73, 112, 114, 116, 119, 123, 134, 135, 136, 167, 182.
Paul, The Apostle   16, 35, 37, 38, 39, 40, 46, 47, 48, 49, 50, 51, 52, 56, 57, 61,, 62, 63, 64, 67, 69, 70, 71, 78, 79, 80, 81, 82, 83, 85, 86, 87, 88, 89, 90, 97, 115, 120, 121, 141, 176.